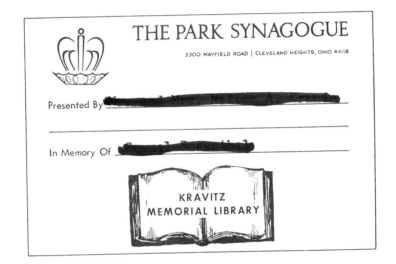

The Art of Judaic Needlework

The Art of Judaic Needlework

Traditional and Contemporary Designs

ITA ABER

CHARLES SCRIBNER'S SONS · NEW YORK

Drawings by Tsirl Waletzky
Photographs by Eve Kessler and Steven Mays
Color plates photographed by Myron Miller

Copyright © 1979 Ita Aber

Library of Congress Cataloging in Publication Data
Aber, Ita H.
The art of Judaic needlework.
Bibliography: p. 145
1. Needlework, Jewish. 2. Decoration and ornament, Jewish.
3. Liturgical objects—Judaism. I. Title
TT750.A17 746.4 '4 79-9050 ISBN 0-684-16239-3

Printed in the United States of America.

Designed by Bobye List.

1 3 5 7 9 11 13 15 17 19 QD/C 20 18 16 14 12 10 8 6 4 2

To Joshua, Mindy, Judah, and Harry . . .
BECAUSE OF YOU

Contents

A color section follows page 86.

PREFACE

My primary reason for writing this book is that some years ago I became aware of the need for a publication on Judaic needlework that would include the works of fine artists, both past and present, and inspire and guide the needle artist at every level of accomplishment. To this end, I have included hard-to-find information such as Hebrew alphabets, calendars, and needlework terms; step-by-step, easy-to-follow instructions and diagrams; a chapter on the curved needle, and one on finishing techniques, because design is only a part of what the needle artist does—of equal importance are craftsmanship, display, and care.

My approach is to define this Jewish art form for our own generation and in our own terms. The jacket front was designed as a contemporary interpretation of a classic theme that is timeless. The Sabbath cloth on the back represents the continuance of an ancient tradition and ritual without which there is no religion. We should be unafraid to express artistically the times in which we live and to pass these expressions along to the next generation in order to encourage their reinterpretation. It is hoped that this book will inspire you and give you much pleasure.

ACKNOWLEDGMENTS   My sincerest thanks go to the many people and organizations who helped me with this project, and through whose kindness the book was made possible: Lavina Abraham, Sophia Adler, Audrey Clayton, Moshe Davidowitz, Ruth Gildesgame, Cora Ginsburg, Ina Golub, Diana Grossman, Joseph P. Horowitz, Erica Jesselson, Peretz Kaminsky, Georgette Mack, Sharon Moskow, Devon Myneder, Julius Schatz, Charles Seliger, Nira and Amiram Shamir, Audry Vinarub, Tsirl Waletzky, Fran Willner, Dorothy Wolken, Professor Yigael Yadin; Cissy Grossman, Joy Ungerleider-Myerson, and Ruth Dolkart of the Jewish Museum, New York; Sylvia Herskowitz of Yeshiva University Museum, New York; Dorothy Kostuch and Florence Lewis May of the Hispanic Society of America, New York; Jean Mailey of the Metropolitan Museum of Art, New York; Aviva Muller-Lancet, Zohar Wilbush, Irene Levitt, and Martin Weil of the Israel Museum, Jerusalem; Rabbi Mitchell Serels of Yeshiva University; Milton Sonday of Cooper-Hewitt Museum, New York; Dr. Susan Wallace Reiling of the Vizcaya Museum and Gardens, Miami, Florida; the Cluny Museum, Paris; the Department of Antiquities, State of Israel, Jerusalem; and the Gannett Newspapers of Westchester, White Plains, New York.

My sincere appreciation to Dr. Irving Greenberg, Susan Fleminger, Moshe Davidowitz, Anita Levine, and Dorothy Kostuch, who read the galleys and offered their help and insight.

Special thanks go to my agent, Julie Fallowfield, my designer, Bobye List, and to Elinor Parker, Carla Packer, Louise Ketz, David Hall, and Patricia Gallagher, of Charles Scribner's Sons, whose sensitivity, positive criticism, and response have been of inestimable value.

I.A.
August 1979

1.
A BRIEF HISTORY OF JUDAIC NEEDLEWORK

THE HISTORY OF Judaic needlework is allied with the history of the Western world. Wherever they went, Jews carried their possessions, and their talents, with them. What has been left to us is a very rich legacy indeed.

A Judaic textile is identified in one of two ways. Generally it is an object that is obviously intended for use in Judaic ritual, such as a torah mantle or a prayer shawl, or it has a designation by Hebrew inscription.

The first recorded mention of embroidery is in the Book of Exodus, Chapter 28, which gives very explicit instructions for the preparation of the garments of the high priest Aaron. It reads: "And they made upon the hem of the robe, pomegranates of blue and purple and scarlet and twined linen, and they made bells of pure gold and put the bells between the pomegranates." There were also specific instructions for making textiles for The Tabernacle. We see from this that needlework is an ancient legacy.

Throughout the Bible rich colors, gold threads, and precious stones are suggested for embroidering and embellishing. Needleworkers were required to create "for splendor and for beauty," as well as "with cunning," and were urged to use all of their creative imagination in the plastic and graphic arts. Careful instructions were given as to what materials should be included and how they should be used. Exodus 28:4 specifically mentions "checker work" (in Hebrew, *tashbetz*), to be used on the garments of the high priest—which design, in the form of checkers, diamond shapes, and quilting, has been made repeatedly in Judaic embroideries over many centuries. Psalm 45:14 states: "Her raiment is of checker work inwrought with gold." These checker designs took the form of bezel settings, as might be used for precious stones. Many surviving embroideries feature lions and lavers and other decorative motifs executed in checker design, often done in red cotton thread on a white ground, such as in eighteenth- and nineteenth-century Purim and Passover hand towels that show this kind of decoration. Checker motifs were, therefore, used successfully in the early Judaic tradition in a variety of ways.

Joseph's "coat of many colors" was really a coat of many stripes. In secular history we are familiar with stripes in the garments of the Greeks, Romans, and Egyptians, the color of the stripe denoting rank. This system continues to apply today; we see it at university graduations, where each faculty member wears a different-colored fold of cloth, called a "hood," which is the shoulder stripe worn to denote degree, university department, or school. Military systems continue to use stripes in various colors and combinations to denote rank and merit.

Chapters 35 to 39 of the Book of Exodus give very definite instructions to Bezalel (whom God had Moses designate to be in charge of construction of the Tabernacle in the wilderness), and to the workers, for the making of the fabrics to be used. Special mention was made of the wisdom of women and the work of embroiderers. It is interesting to note that Bezalel is a Hebrew name that comes from *B'tzale El*, "under the shadow [or protection] of God." Bezalel is filled with *Chochma, Bina, v'Daat* (the contraction is *chabad*), ". . . and he put together what everyone else had prepared and together with his assistant Aholiab . . ." There is no other single artistic enterprise mentioned in the Bible as being under divine protection. From this we know that the plastic and graphic artist held a singular position in the Jewish community. What is most extraordinary is that while the people of Israel were still in the desert, they prepared all of the materials for the making of the Tabernacle. They were even asked to stop, because too much had been prepared!

Several verses of the aforementioned Exodus chapters state that only "wise-hearted people" should be involved: ". . . every man and woman whose heart made them willing to bring all manner of work, which the Lord had commanded them to be made"; and, again: ". . . every wise-hearted man, in whom the Lord had put wisdom and understanding to know how to do every manner of work for the service of the sanctuary." We learn from this that both men and women were embroiderers, weavers, and, in fact, artists of every type. "Willing-hearted" men brought precious metals, and "wise-hearted" women spun with their hands.

The earliest-known Judaic textile fragments that remain to us come from the cave of the ancient hero Bar Kochba, which dates from the years 132–35 C.E. (Common Era). The weavings—in red, green, purple, gold, and multicolored stripes of every variety—were dyed in a most sophisticated manner; indeed, a total of thirty-four color varieties were found. They are located today in the collection of the Shrine of the Book in Jerusalem. We know the textiles are Jewish from the solid stripes woven into them, familiar to us over the centuries from the *talit,* or prayer shawl.

The solid stripe of the *talit* is seen again in the frescos of the synagogue at Dura Europus (256 C.E.), which is located in Syria and was excavated in 1932 by Yale University archaeologists. (Yeshiva University Museum, New York, has both large- and small-scale models of it on view to the public.) The solid stripe, woven in various colors to denote rank, is also seen in purple: a color reserved for royalty. In the frescos every segment of the murals features textiles of one sort or another; the garments of the figures depicted have stripes and fringes that are clearly visible. Draped cornices, held by human figures to enclose specific scenes, resemble decorations seen on torah binders much later in Jewish history. In one scene of the Temple of Aaron there is a draped fabric veil in the process of being removed to unveil the interior; this curtain is the first visual record we have of such a Judaic textile.

Early striped toga-like garments had ritual fringes at the four corners. The Talmud says that Joseph's coat of many stripes was a prayer shawl of a long, rectangular shape with fringes at the corners. In the Dura Europus frescos we begin to see the round garments, a type of pantaloon, that were then coming into vogue. This led to the creation of a separate *talit* for the wearing of ritual fringes. The *talit katan,* or small *talit,* was created as a convenience in the late talmudic and early medieval period.

We have little information on Judaic textiles from the period of mosaic-designed synagogues in the early part of our Common Era to the much later Golden Age of Spain in the thirteenth century. It is known, however, that in Persia during the years 629–45 C.E., Jews were involved in all manner of crafts and fine arts, including the weaving and dyeing of linen and wool, needlework, tapestry weaving, and tailoring and leather crafting. According to the late Mark Wischnitzer, in *A History of Jewish Crafts and Guilds,* "Jewish artists knew how to weave fine brocaded silks, woolen stuffs, carpets and so on." He goes on to tell us that the Jews in Baghdad, Egypt, Sicily, and Spain were, for a thousand years, involved in every area of the textile industry, including the raising of silkworms. Flavius Josephus, in his celebrated *History of the Jewish War,* mentions a market for woolen goods in the New City of Jerusalem. The synagogue of the "tarsiim" in Jerusalem belonged to the weavers of "tarsian" cloth. In Lydda there was a synagogue of weavers.

The Temple in Jerusalem, rebuilt by Herod, boasted a "Babylonian curtain" in its interior, separating the sanctuary from the Holy of Holies. Josephus describes it in detail: "It was embroidered with blue and fine linen and scarlet and purple, and of a contexture that was truly wonderful." He interprets the colors as symbolic of the four elements. Some astronomical designs were included on it: ". . . all that was to be seen in the heavens, except for the signs of the zodiac."

The Temple administration, along with the court of the king, was one of the largest employers of labor. Masons, carpenters, goldsmiths and other metal workers, embroiderers, and weavers were constantly engaged in repairing buildings and utensils. Another source mentions that women weavers working on the repair of the Temple curtains were paid from the Temple's building funds. In the Syriac Apocalypse of Baruch, there are references to young and unmarried women engaged in weaving. However, weaving was in the main a man's occupation.

When the artisan passed through the city or went to a nearby village, he was recognized by the distinctive badge that he wore. The tailor had a needle stuck in the front of his dress; the wool carder showed a woolen thread; the dyer carried different-colored threads from which patrons could select the desired shade; the weaver carried a small distaff behind his ear.

The textile crafts embraced a whole group of trades: the raising of sheep; the cultivation of hemp; the weaving of wool, linen, and silk; fulling; dyeing; washing; sewing; and so on. Palestinian textile production made marked progress in the first centuries of the Common Era. It has been rightly stressed that while fabrics, such as those used for the garments of the high priests, used to be imported from Egypt or India during the period of the Second Commonwealth, Palestine itself at this time produced such fabrics for export. Both talmudic and non-Jewish sources point to the excellent textiles of Beth Shean.

Silk weaving flourished in Upper Galilee, the township of Giscalah being renowned for it; the silk fabricated there was sold in the markets of Tyre. Long before the reign of Emperor Justinian (527–65 C.E.), silk yarn from China and India reached Palestine, where it was woven. It has been suggested that Jews purchased the silk yarn from caravans passing through Aqaba from the East on their way to Gaza, then interwove the silk and wool and exported the finished fabrics to the West.

Unfortunately, all traces of the actual textiles manufactured during this period have disappeared, though, as seen, the industry is referred to by sources not only in Palestine but also in Egypt and Asia Minor in the talmudic period. Indeed, in fourth-century Egypt, curtains embroidered with fantastic figures were known as "Vela Judaica"—indicating the significant Jewish influence.

During the Middle Ages, eastern Jews migrated west in the wake of the Arab invasion of North Africa. These migrations to southern Europe brought them to Italy, southern France, Spain, and the Balkans.

A Hispano-Moresque rug (Illustration 1) dated 1450, in the collection of the Vizcaya Museum and Gardens in Miami, Florida, features several borders around a ground of six-pointed stars intertwined in classical Islamic motif. One outer border depicts stylized pomegranates, a five-branch candelabrum, and individual six-pointed stars, while the inner

1. Details of a fifteenth-century Hispano-Moresque rug. The Deering Collection, Vizcaya Museum and Gardens, Miami, Florida.

border, next to it, features lions and lambs, birds of several varieties, and what looks like cuneiform writing. Since the menorah is by far the most important single Judaic symbol, it seems reasonable to assume that the rug was made for a Judaic purpose. From its size it might have been for a synagogue floor. A companion rug, in disintegrated condition, is in the collection of the Metropolitan Museum of Art in New York.

There are also fragments of this type of rug in the collection of the Hispanic Society of America in New York and in the Textile Museum in Washington, D.C. Jewish textile fragments of the Spanish period may be found in the collection of the State Jewish Museum in Prague. It houses the world's largest collection of Judaic textiles and embroideries, while the Jewish Museum in New York houses the most diverse collection in the world. The Textile Museum in Washington has a rug dating from the second quarter of the fifteenth century featuring the arms of the Enríquez family, who were known Marranos, and the arms of the de Rojas family, who were known Conversos.

During the Golden Age of Spain, needlework, rug making, and lace making reached their highest degree of excellence. Cecil Roth tells us that the Jews and the Moors excelled in these areas. It is believed that examples of the outstanding skill of Jewish and Moorish lacemakers were carried to Italy in the fifteenth century. These dentelles arabes ("Arab laces") spread throughout Europe, and the high quality of sixteenth-century Italian lace—among the finest in the world—may be attributed to Jewish and Moslem skill.

Although most Moslems, when expelled from Spain in 1492, emigrated to Africa, most Jews fled to other countries. Throughout Europe and the Middle East, the fine-quality carpets and brocaded textiles that began to appear during this period are believed to have been an important contribution of these expelled peoples. After the expulsion of the Jews and Moslems, a dramatic change in the style of Spanish rugs is evident. It follows that the improved quality of rugs and other crafts in Europe and Africa was doubtless a direct result of the migration of these peoples.

An article in *Embroidery* magazine, London, written many years ago, deals with "Armenian, Jewish or Arab Lace." We find here that the lace patterns closely resemble Palestinian embroidery patterns as well as patterns from *Dentelles et Broderies Tunisiennes,* published in Paris in 1931. Palestinians and Israelis have continued to be lacemakers. In addition, designs from North African carpets and textiles have the same geometric qualities and stitch count as some of the lace and have an appearance similar to Palestinian embroidery as well. Many examples of this lace, in similar geometric design, appear in *Hispanic Lace and Lace Making,* by Florence Lewis May, published by the Hispanic Society of America.

When the Jews fled Spain they carried with them their precious possessions, including their beautiful handwoven fabrics, brocades, and embroideries. The sumptuary laws forbade leaving their textiles in Spain.

The precious embroideries taken from Spain of course wore out with the passage of time and with use, and were cut up, the good portions saved. These beautiful fragments would be included, with tender loving care, in new torah mantles, ark curtains, and other ritual objects; they were laid-in in appliqué or cartouche style onto brocade or embroidered surfaces. Even before the expulsion, valuable fragments of old Judaic embroidery had been so used, on fifteenth-century Italian velvet brocade. Reds and blues dominated these early velvet brocades, and there has been much green included in Judaic ritual objects. The predominating patterns of the fragments which were laid-in were stylizations of the blossom and fruit of the pomegranate. This was an important symbol to Christians, as it was to Jews. A stylized artichoke design was also favored.

As a Jewish symbol, the pomegranate is recognized as one of the most perfect spheres in nature. As a symbol of fertility and plenty, it is one of the so-called "seven species." It is also supposed to come close to

Left: 2. Church hanging, Italy, 1480. Cut-velvet brocade of pomegranates and twisted vines. Courtesy of the Hispanic Society of America, New York.   Right: 3. Panel, cut voided velvet brocade. Metropolitan Museum of Art, New York, bequest of George Blumenthal, 1941.

having 613 seeds, representing the number of commandments referred to in the Bible. Because the pomegranate was so loved by so many people, it was not unusual that this pattern in exotic silk velvet brocade would be used for synagogue, as well as church, decoration. A fabric dated 1480 in the State Jewish Museum in Prague, shown as Illustration 4, has a companion church hanging in the collection of the Hispanic Society of America (Illustration 2). A similar fragment is in the collection of the Textile Study Room at the Metropolitan Museum of Art (Illustration 3). It is known that these were of Italian origin.

Sometimes the precious fragments of Jewish textiles brought from Spain were set in the new torah mantle in a cartouche or bezel setting, as if they were jewels. Some of these were made of silk, fully embroidered and set with these saved fragments, using another variety of embroidery to finish the bottom, and had fringes applied to epaulets and openings. Very beautiful indeed! A masterpiece of this type (Illustration 5) can be seen in the Jewish Museum in New York; it has green cut velvet inserts laid on a pink silk ground embroidered, petit point-style, onto the silk with multicolored silk- and metal-thread embroidery. The bottom design

Left: 4. Ark curtain of velvet brocade, Florence, Italy, 1480. Courtesy of the State Jewish Museum, Prague.   Right: 5. Torah mantle, Italy, late seventeenth century. Green cut- and uncut-velvet fragments set onto pink silk embroidered with petit point flowers and metal threads. Courtesy of the Benguiat Family Collection, the Jewish Museum, New York.

of the mantle is in classic Chinese design. The diagonal border bands symbolize water for the Chinese, but for us they are simply beautiful. As we know, Jews were often traveling merchants, and it does seem reasonable to assume that they would have brought back handsome embroideries for decorating their synagogues, as well as for dresses for their brides; most certainly they were influenced by these exotic embroideries, which found their way into synagogue decoration—for the glory of God as well as for ornamentation.

It is known that bride's dresses in Europe were eventually recut and reused for torah-mantle and ark-curtain needleworks. Just as fragments of the fifteenth-century velvets were used as insertions, so were saved fragments of beautiful bride's dresses. While the mantle and ark curtain mentioned earlier are known to have been made in Italy in the seventeeth century, the velvet inserts may well have been made in an earlier century.

By the end of the seventeenth century, European Jewish women, confined more and more to their homes, entered a long period of three hundred years of dreary ghetto confinement. The degradations of life outside the home could be put aside, however, and their lives made more cheerful when they did their needlework. During this time an increased coarsening of yarns is evident in the examples remaining, reflecting oppression by their host countries; but their work generally remained superb in skill. The first physician to define occupational diseases was Bernardino Ramazzini, a professor of medicine at Padua. He was a gentile who wrote in 1700 about Jewish needlewomen and how they stood at open windows in all seasons to use the daylight for their work. This resulted in innumerable respiratory ailments and in eyesight that often failed completely before they reached the age of forty. An Italian *me shebayrach* blessing of the seventeenth century, read in synagogue on the Sabbath of the week in which a new needlework was presented to the synagogue, states: ". . . the One who blessed our mothers, Sarah, Rebecca, Rachel, and Leah, may He give His blessings to every daughter of Israel who makes a mantle or cloth for the honor of the Torah, may the Lord reward and remunerate her and let us say amen." This blessing continues to be used in the classic tradition in synagogues when handiworks are presented to the sanctuary.

Evidence exists that a Jew was an embroiderer at the court of Prussia in the year Ramazzini wrote. Further evidence indicates that in the eighteenth century a Bohemian Jew worked for the Episcopal court in Fulda as artistic gold embroiderer for missal robes and other clerical vestments, and that a Jew executed embroideries for the Emperor of Germany. All of the aforementioned shows that the old textile arts mentioned in the Bible continued to flourish even while Jewish oppression increased.

Nevertheless, the Jews' seclusion from the rest of the European community did not permit a free exchange of ideas and it was difficult for the creative artist to grow. In all areas of creative art pursued by the European Jews there was a lessening of skill as materials became, of necessity, poorer and cruder. Creative needlework did continue to flourish for synagogue and home decoration, but its materials were not as fine and the work was now somewhat coarse. The guilds, including the needlework one, did not admit Jewish members (and, because they were church-sponsored, with patron saints, Jewish artists would not have joined them), although it is known that in Prague in 1741 a Society of Jewish Embroiderers and Tailors thrived; a woodcut shows the members of the society parading with their banners.

Despite their difficulties, Jewish people had almost always worked at handcrafts. When Jewish women could not participate directly in religious synagogue services, they may have felt apart from what was happening around them. However, they could actively participate by beautifying the interiors of their homes and houses of worship with all manner of embroideries and other handiwork. Needlework was a fine art as well as a personal expression of skill; it was, therefore, common for needleworkers to sign and date their work. It followed an earlier tradition, seen in excavated synagogues—where names and dedications were included in the structure—that artists should sign, date, and dedicate their work. This practice is continued today.

The use of symbols and traditional designs that gave importance to every act of Jewish ritual at home was an expression of their religious life and a means for women, as well as men, to uplift a mundane existence. The mezuzah (doorpost parchment) at the threshold led to a special Jewish world. A strong Moslem influence affected the symbology of Jews in Middle Eastern countries and in Africa, just as a Christian influence made itself felt in European countries. As a result, the symbols so familiar in the Russian pale are generally not seen among the works of the Jews of North Africa and the Mediterranean. There is no doubt that the cultural influence of the countries in which they lived reflected itself in their designs and customs.

The symbols used by early Jewish embroiderers in Europe had represented things that were familiar to them, especially the religious objects of Judaism. Wine cups, Sabbath breads, and candles were very familiar objects. From silver and brass ceremonial objects they took the Tablets, the tree of life, the *magen* David (shield or star of David), twisted columns, lions, crowns, and a host of other symbols. These were not used very much in the early years after the Expulsion from Spain, but when ghetto and *shtetl* (Jewish town or village) life became entrenched, these motifs again came into common use. Their use was at its height in the late nineteenth and early twentieth centuries.

While fine-art embroidery was practiced all over the world and by many different groups of people who achieved great heights of proficiency, the Jewish community is responsible for several types of work that are not seen in other ethnic or regional groups of embroiderers.

The first is the torah binder, also called a wrapper or wimpel, which is an exclusively Jewish embroidery expression. Another particularly Jewish embroidery expression is *Spanier arbeit* ("Spanish work") used for *atarot* (neckbands for the prayer shawl) and *Brusttuke* (chest bib) for brides, as well as for skullcaps. There is little information on how *Spanier arbeit* was actually made, although it is known that it is a combination weaving and embroidery technique. Many examples exist in Jewish museums, but many are in disrepair. This work was made in Russia for several centuries, and later in Berdyczew and Radziwill. In the latter part of the nineteenth century the work was done in Sasow in Galicia. *Spanier arbeit* is executed with silver or gold heavy thread wrapped around cotton cords.

Another kind of embroidery rarely seen in secular work but often in synagogue needlework is heavy three-dimensional embroidery. Beginning in the seventeenth century, German Jewish women created this needlework that is still cherished today, when it can be found. Two well-known Jewish men, master embroiderers, were Jacob Koppel Gans, who was a master *Goldsticker,* and Elkanah of Naubmey, who did impressive ark curtains with gold and silver thread on deep-colored velvet in a heavy, raised, three-dimensional embroidery. Such heavy three-dimensional embroideries were classically made for ark curtains and torah mantles as well as valances. The symbols used were made and appliquéd to a solid fabric ground. Hebrew letters were sometimes cut out of craft paper, covered in metal threads, and were then applied (Illustrations 6 and 7).

Pearlwork and embroidery was also known as a Jewish trade throughout Europe. Christian ecclesiastical embroideries with pearlwork

Left: 6. Ark curtain, Bavaria, 1772–73, by Jacob Koppel Gans, goldsticker. Made of green velvet with red and buff cut and uncut velvet. Embroidered with heavy metal threads in three-dimensional embroidery. Courtesy of the Friedman Collection, the Jewish Museum, New York.   Right: 7. Detail of ark curtain valance, showing three-dimensional embroidery appliqué and metal thread-covered craft paper letters. Courtesy of the Danzig Collection, the Jewish Museum, New York.

are seen in France from the sixteenth, seventeenth, and eighteenth centuries. Examples of this work are to be found in many European churches and museums. Embroideries were also decorated with fish scales, glass baubles, and semiprecious stones. Saragossa's Jewish craftsmen had gentiles among their customers. The royal court employed quite a number of tailors and pearlworkers. In 1347, the pearlworker Gadella Avenarama obtained through King Pedro IV two seats for himself and his descendants in the synagogue at Calatayud, thus circumventing the synagogue board.

From the seventeenth century onward, we find a variety of torah binders from many European countries. The largest group are from Germany, where they were called wimpels. Originally the swaddling cloth of the infant male, and used at his circumcision, the cloth was laundered, cut into four strips, and sewn together into a long, narrow binder. It was then embroidered, or sometimes painted, with the name of the child and the Hebrew date of birth. Many of these cloths stated: "Born under a good sign," referring to the zodiac sign, and included the blessing that the child should grow up to *torah* (bar mitzvah), *chuppah* (marriage), and *maasim tovim* (performance of good deeds). They often ended with the words "Amen, Selah, may it be the will of the Lord." The binder was presented to the synagogue when the child was three, dry in his pants, and ready for the study of his prayers and the Bible. The embroidered binders included innovative use of the Hebrew alphabet, as well as animals, birds, people, and patriotic symbols. They can be compared to the American sampler, for as they piled up in the holy arks of Europe, they became an authentic history of the families of the region and a Who's Who of the Jewish community.

Torah binders from Italy, North Africa, and the Middle East were not made from circumcision cloths; they were beautiful embroideries with dedicatory inscriptions, often presented to the synagogue to honor a person or special occasion. These binders appear to have been made either by professional embroiderers or by highly skilled craftspersons, whereas the German wimpels were folk-art embroideries.

Yemenite embroidery—so desirable and so beautiful—was made by both men and women, and was used for clothing only. The distinctive geometric patterns resemble Palestinian and other Eastern needleworks, but their use of gold- and silver-metal threads, couched in circular designs, with a colored thread, was always uniquely theirs and unmistakable. These much-sought-after treasures are a distinctly unique contribution of the Jewish needleworkers of San'a, Yemen.

Top: 8. Torah binders. The top one is from Italy, 1602; the middle one from Germany, 1737; and the bottom ones are (left) from Germany, 1829, and (right) Germany, 1718. Courtesy of the Israel Museum, Jerusalem.   Bottom: 9. Torah binder, Italy, seventeenth century. Embroidery on lace. Courtesy of the Rothschild-Strauss Collection, Cluny Museum, Paris.

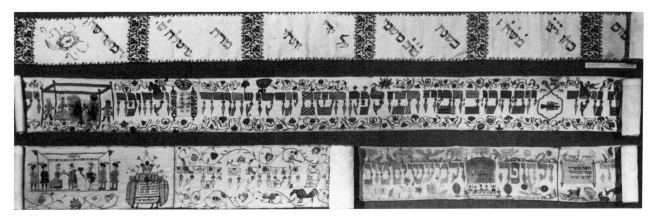

Top: 10. Torah binder. Detail of a binder from eastern Germany, 1762. It is made of undyed linen embroidered with silk. Courtesy of the Friedman Collection, the Jewish Museum, New York. Center: 11. Torah binder, Italy, seventeenth century. Flowers on a dark blue ground are worked in gold and blue on linen canvas, 9′4″ long × 6¼″ wide. Courtesy of Cora Ginsburg. Bottom: 12. Torah binder, Italy, late-sixteenth or early-seventeenth century. Blue silk embroidery on cream linen. Courtesy of Cora Ginsburg.

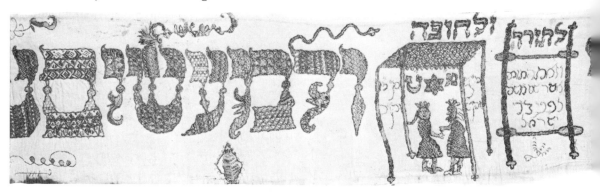

With the advent of the sewing machine in 1855 and the subsequent standardization of clothing sizes in the 1860s (during the period of the American Civil War), the European Jewish community became increasingly involved in the needle trades. They found their way to the United States and prospered at their ancient work. By the 1940s, more than 340,000 people were involved in the needle trades in New York City alone. The Jewish community predominated in this industry as they did elsewhere in the United States, Canada, and England.

Over the years, the finest secular fabric crafts had moved out of the home into ateliers and studios, finally becoming industrialized by the machine making of lace and embroideries. The home-woven tapestry had evolved to Aubussons and Gobelins in France, now being done in Puerto Rico, Mexico, and the Orient to reduce cost. But with the machine age heavily upon us, there has been a resurgence of handwork as we are each trying to find again that quality of life we once knew and to define it in our own terms.

The twentieth-century Judaic classical embroidery motifs of lions and crowns that predominate on velvet, in jewel tones, is going out of style. The lions were so popular because they represented the Israelite tribe of Judah, the largest of the tribes, whose symbol is the lion. We have also seen much use of the hands of the *kohanim* (priests), as well as of lavers—representing the Levites (those who wash the hands of the priests). These classically simple but highly commercial needleworks continued to be used until the period of World War II, and while they are still being made today, they are being used less frequently.

In recent years, a small number of well-known artists have made wonderful designs for synagogue needlework, and their work has been very successful. Unfortunately, many American embroiderers today are not well schooled in Judaism and/or craftsmanship and design. This is reflected in the large quantity of inferior materials that have been produced. As a result, the decoration of contemporary synagogues often seems to stop after the architect has selected the carpet color (too often beige or rust) and the pillows for the benches, although in some cases the synagogue committee will go so far as to match the ark curtain or the torah mantles with the carpet. It is surprising how rarely anyone on a synagogue committee thinks beyond these basic decisions.

Jews were never truly part of the melting pot. They may have surrounded themselves with contemporary trappings, but their rituals have always been the same. Home and synagogue are paramount, as is the study of Torah; and the role of women is virtually the same. Everything in life is cyclical, and the role of women is evolving to the sensible values that existed from biblical times through the eleventh century in Spain. Today, however, since the establishment of the State of Israel after the Holocaust, these traditions and symbols are evolving into contemporary designs with bright colors that evoke the loud singing of praises. Accompanying the return to the original biblical language and land is a return to biblical symbols, motifs, and representations. I hope here, in this book, to urge a return to these basic religious expressions and to add some new ones representing expressions of our own times—bold new symbols executed in bold colors that make positive statements and a positive commitment.

2.
YOUR FIRST PROJECT

* ═══════════════════════════════════════ *

A Jewish Sampler

MATERIALS

* Paper
* Pencil
* *The Comprehensive Hebrew Calendar,* by Arthur Spier (see Bibliography)
* Hebrew Bible with English translations
* Hebrew alphabet designs (taken from Chapter Eleven of this book)
* Graph paper
* Muslin
* Canvas *or* linen/cotton
* Needle (curved; see Chapter Fourteen)
* Varieties of cotton, linen, silk, or wool thread
* Artist's stretcher (for use with canvas) or embroidery hoop (for use with linen/cotton)
* Staple gun and staples (for affixing canvas to stretcher)
* Additional materials as may be needed (mentioned in this chapter)

13. STANDARD HEBREW ALEPHBET WITH NUMERICAL VALUES.

5	4	3	2	2	1
ה	ד	ג	ב	בּ	א
Has the sound of H	Has the sound of D	Has the sound of G	Has the sound of V	Has the sound of B	Silent letter
20	**10**	**9**	**8**	**7**	**6**
כ	י	ט	ח	ז	ו
Has the sound of K	Has the sound of Y	Has the sound of T	Has the sound of H	Has the sound of Z	Has the sound of V
50	**40**	**40**	**30**	**20**	**20**
נ	ם	מ	ל	ך	כּ
Has the sound of N	Has the sound of M At the end of a word	Has the sound of M	Has the sound of L	Has the sound of H At the end of a word	Has the sound of H
80	**80**	**80**	**70**	**60**	**50**
ף	פ	פּ	ע	ס	ן
Has the sound of F At the end of a word	Has the sound of F	Has the sound of P	Silent letter	Has the sound of S	Has the sound of N At the end of a word
300	**300**	**200**	**100**	**90**	**90**
שׂ	שׁ	ר	ק	ץ	צ
Has the sound of S	Has the sound of SH	Has the sound of R	Has the sound of K	Has the sound of TZ At the end of a word	Has the sound of TZ
Has the sound of E as in "bell"	Has the sound of A SFARDI E as in "bell"	Has the sound of A as in "father"	Has the sound of A as in tell SFARDI A as in "father"	**400** ת	**400** תּ
				Has the sound of S SFARDI T	Has the sound of T
Has the sound of O as in "no" SFARDI AW	Has the sound of OO as in "moon"	Has the sound of EE	Has no sound		

14. Top: The Hebrew months, lunisolar or Babylonian agricultural calendar.
Bottom: The biblical calendar, including the zodiac.

TISHRE _____ תִּשְׁרִי

CHESHVAN _____ חשון

KISLEV_____ כִּסְלֵו

TEVET _____ טֵבֵת

SHEVAT _____ שְׁבַט

ADAR _____ אֲדָר

NISSAN _____ נִיסָן

IYAR _____ אִייָר

SIVAN _____ סִיוָן

TAMUZ _____ תַּמּוּז

AV _____ אָב

ELUL _____ אֱלוּל

Hebrew Month	Corresponding English Date	Zodiac
Nissan	March 21–April 19	Aries
Iyar	April 20–May 20	Taurus
Sivan	May 21–June 21	Gemini
Tamuz	June 22–July 21	Cancer
Av	July 22–August 21	Leo
Elul	August 22–September 22	Virgo
Tishri	September 23–October 22	Libra
Cheshvan	October 23–November 21	Scorpio
Kislev	November 22–December 21	Sagittarius
Tevet	December 22–January 19	Capricorn
Shevat	January 20–February 18	Aquarius
Adar	February 19–March 20	Pisces

There are two months of Adar in a leap year. The Roman dates are approximate. Nissan is the first month of the biblical calendar year, which is spring to spring. Tishri is the first month of the lunisolar or Babylonian agricultural calendar. The fifteenth of Shevat is the new calendar year for the growing of trees.

Sunday—day *aleph*   Monday—day *beth*   Tuesday—day *gimel*
Wednesday—day *daled*   Thursday—day *hey*   Friday—day *vav*
Saturday—Sabbath

Accumulate ideas in a folder. These ideas may be in the form of doodlings or drawings, photos, swatches of fiber and fabric, found objects, pressed flowers and leaves, an inspirational phrase, or a note to jog the memory about something. The gathered ideas should be given time to jell. When you finally go through these materials, you may discard some, save some for other projects, change your idea of what the present project will be, add new things, or generally overhaul the concept. All this helps you to be reassured about how the project will proceed and be handled. To begin, I suggest that a drawing or cartoon of the design be prepared, along with color ideas.

Use a piece of muslin as a doodle cloth. The muslin should be washed with soap in order to remove the sizing, and then should be washed a second time without soap in order to remove any soap residue. You will then have a piece of material that is completely inert and free of foreign matter. This doodle cloth is a practice piece that can eventually become a sampler of design ideas, stitches, and color concepts. You should keep a notebook of ideas and procedures, of course, but the doodle cloth is where you will experiment, make mistakes, and make your corrections. When some of your initial designing has been executed on the doodle cloth—which is held in a hoop—you may decide that you want to make your sampler on canvas rather than on linen. The choice is simple and the choice is yours. Once you are satisfied with the way a stitch or a design looks on the doodle cloth, you can then do the work directly onto the permanent surface to be embellished.

Left: 15. Sampler, United States, 1830. Light blue, green, rose, and white embroidery on unbleached linen. Made by Rachel Seixas and bequeathed to Nellie Cardozo. Courtesy of the Friedman Collection, the Jewish Museum, New York. Right: 16. American sampler, 1787. It features classic sampler techniques in the Philadelphia style, including a Hebrew alphabet. Courtesy of Devon Myneder.

The beginning embroiderer can do very successful work using simple stitches, and, with time, those simple stitches can be added to. The finest embroideries, including ecclesiastical ones, in museums today are what we call "single-stitch embroideries." They are made completely with a single stitch—either a simple split stitch, chain stitch, or long-and-short stitch. The knowledge of a lot of stitches is therefore not really necessary for successful embroidery.

Whatever design you finally decide to use—whether it is something here in this book, something you have created yourself, or something you had an artist create for you—a simple split-stitch or chain outline can be very successful by itself. You can, of course, embellish it.

A split stitch is similar to a running stitch, except that you go back and split through the stitch; your back stitch is also a running stitch. The chain stitch is very dressy, and can make something very simple look very formal, as though a lot of work has gone into it. The chain stitch is simple to execute. You will note in the chapter on Passover (Six) that the chain stitch is used to outline some of the Hebrew lettering—a very effective and successful technique. The single chain of a chain-stitch design is sometimes called a lazy daisy. It is an excellent fill-in stitch, ideal for flowers.

A good way to begin working on a Judaic embroidery sampler is to find out your Hebrew given name. Then find out your Hebrew date of birth, which will tell you what portion of the Bible was read during the week that you were born. Suddenly you have a highly personalized portion of the Bible that belongs to you. Each of us has a day on which we were born and on which God created something. We also have a zodiac symbol and a constellation, the rabbinic interpretations of which are fascinating. Possibly starting with no ideas for design, quite unexpectedly you will find that you have a variety of symbols from which to choose to begin your sampler.

Write out your first name in Hebrew letters. It is advisable, in order to encourage more design in the embroidery, that you make the first letter of your name about three times as large as the rest of your name. This will allow you to fill in and decorate it with all kinds of interesting designs. You might decide to pick symbols from your profession or hobby. You might include a family seal that you like, a family saying, or an idea that is of special interest to you. Biblical references can include flowers, fauna, birds, people, ideas, concepts, colors, precious stones, etc., plus sayings, all of which may be interpreted in the sampler in whatever fashion pleases you.

 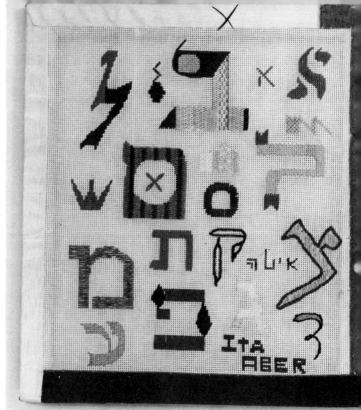

17. and 18. Two Hebrew samplers depicting ideas for Hebrew lettering. (See Color Plate 17.) The sampler in Illustration 17 (left) is made on muslin and the one in Illustration 18 (right) is made on canvas. Made by Ita Aber.

19. Sampler of two designs made up of several Hebrew letters conjoined and decorated. It is worked in a classic manuscript illumination concept. Made by Ita Aber.

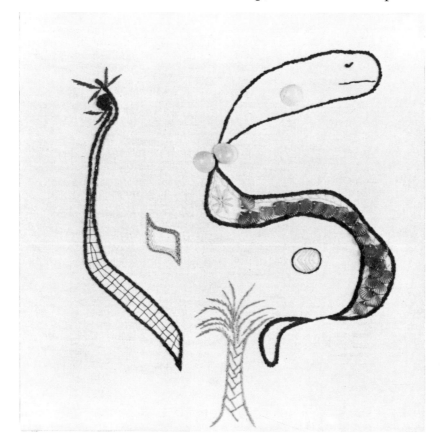

It is very common in Jewish history for us to sign our names to the things that we have made or been involved with. Many archaeological discoveries carry the names of the people who worked on them, the names of those who were honored for their community efforts, and the names of the donors. This ancient tradition continues in our own times with dedications and plaques used in Jewish centers, synagogues, and schools. We see it on the backs of many of the chairs in the chapels where we pray, and we also see it on our embroideries.

The early embroideries left to us have wonderful dedications that read: "Made for the glory of God" or "Made for the honor of God," and even, for example, "Contributed and given by the very gentle woman and her very gentle husband." There were sometimes encoded messages worked into the letters of the dedications. It was appropriate when a new torah mantle or ark curtain was presented to the synagogue, often the work of some of the ladies in the community, that a special prayer of blessing was said to thank them for their work; the work was, of course, always signed and dated.

In working out your first sampler, you are perhaps learning the use of the Hebrew alphabet, and you are learning to see your own name in embroidery. Perhaps you might want to work out a logo or hallmark—a sign that is specifically yours. (This sign is also called an "artist's chop.") It consists of one or more letters, signs, or symbols that become your own personal symbol. This is truly in the Judaic tradition and may be included in your sampler along with the stitchery as you learn new stitches, use fibers that you have never used before in different colors, and of course implement different styles of Hebrew lettering. This will then truly be a Judaic sampler.

We find in our contemporary society that almost everyone is wearing someone else's name. Couturiers' names are being worn by all the fashionable people, but there is no reason why we cannot wear our own names! We know how important names really are and that while they are very personal, people like to see them written down. That is why there are charity fund-raising journals in which a page is donated with the inscription "In honor of . . ." or "Best wishes from . . ." This is also in the Judaic tradition.

There are charts of the Hebrew alphabet elsewhere in this book—see Chapter Eleven—as well as ideas there for adapting Roman letters to Hebrew letters. Take a look and see what you can use. I would also like to suggest that you get a copy of *How the Hebrew Language Grew,* by Edward

Horowitz. You may also want to see the book by Ben Shahn, *The Alphabet of Creation*. (For both, see the Bibliography.) On your sampler, try to work each letter of your name in a different style of Hebrew lettering, so that later you will be able to use different styles of alphabet design in your embroidery.

20. A logo, also known as a hallmark or a chop, is an artist's trademark. Below are sample logos that include the logo © of The Pomegranate Guild of Judaic Needlework.

21. Logo of Ben Shahn, featuring the Hebrew alphabet conjoined. Copyright © Estate of Ben Shahn, 1978.

It is traditional in needlework to use either fabric or canvas, because each material is merely another woven surface that can be embellished with your embroidery stitches. For a first sampler, it is often fun to use even-weave linen or hardanger fabric, because each can be treated both as a canvas and as a regular embroidery surface. You will discover as you work on them that all kinds of stitchery are adaptable to both surfaces. You can count threads as you do on a canvas, or you can embroider them as you might a piece of crewel work.

Once your design has been worked out on paper and you have doodled your intended embroidery stitches on the doodle cloth, you are ready to execute your design on the permanent fabric, whether it is canvas, cotton, or linen.

Begin by darkening the design on paper with a black marking pen. You must not use any marking pen on your fabric. The reason is very simple: Pens that are not waterproof will bleed through your embroidery when it is blocked or when it is washed. Even waterproof pens tend to absorb and spread at different rates on fabrics, so that the embroiderer cannot achieve a fine line. Moreover, the long-term effects of the synthetic materials and chemicals found in waterproof pens are still unknown.

There are several methods for transferring your design onto the fabric. One is to take the paper with the design on it and tape it to a window in bright daylight. Then tape your fabric over it. The design can then be traced onto the fabric with a number two pencil. It is preferable, however, to make yourself a light box (Illustration 22). This consists of a sheet of glass, supported at both ends by some books, with a small light placed underneath. Put your paper design onto the glass, and lay the fabric on top of the design. If you're careful, you need not tape the fabric—and because there will be no tape residue, this is a more satisfactory method. You can then trace the design with a number two pencil, or, better still, use a single-thread running stitch, which is removable. Use a contrasting color thread.

Left: 22. Homemade light box, made of a piece of glass, supported at both ends with books and a light set underneath.   Right: 23. Homemade light box with design and fabric placed over, showing the use of the curved needle and thread for outlining.

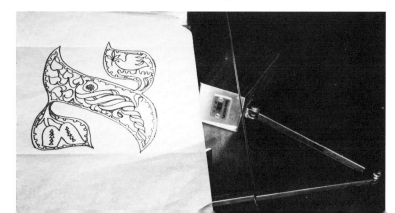
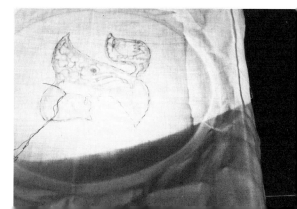

If you want to take your design from a small drawing, you might take that drawing and trace it onto a piece of Mylar plastic with a black grease pencil. You then make a photographic slide out of it, put the slide into a projector, and project it onto a wall at the desired size. Then tape a piece of paper onto the wall and trace the design onto the paper with a black marking pen. It is a simple matter, then, to transfer the design from the paper to the fabric, either with a number two lead pencil or with the running-stitch technique.

Left: 24. Flower design for a young woman who believed in "flower power." Right: 25. Hebrew name for the sampler *Chaya* expresses the idea that this young woman is studying law, is an avid reader, wants peace for the whole world, and talks very well.

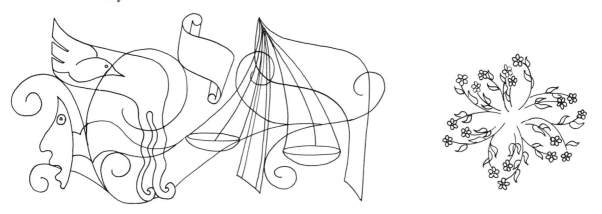

26. Sampler of *Chaya* being worked on hardanger fabric with cotton floss and cotton perle. The sampler was treated as a canvas and as a regular fabric surface. The flower, reminder of an old nickname, was included. Courtesy of Mindy Ann Aber.

27. Assorted decorated letters that adapt to embroidery and fine canvaswork.

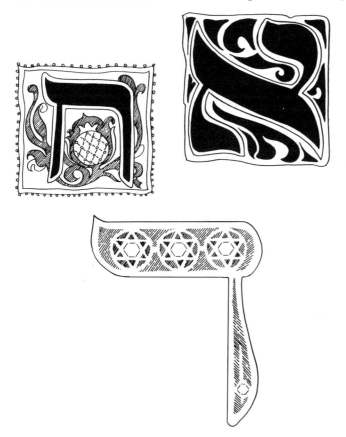

If you use a pencil tracing, it is a good idea to reinforce it with a single-thread running-stitch outline. Not only is the thread removed easily but it remains until removed, whereas pencil lead sometimes rubs off while you are working the piece. Sometimes pencil markings remain in the work; if so, they can be washed out easily at a future date.

If you used a thread for tracing instead of a pencil, should you make a mistake, you simply remove the thread and rework the design outline again.

It is interesting to note that old torah binders were often outlined in some form of india ink. They were embroidered with wool fibers that were subsequently eaten by moths. Underneath, the outline still remains. In other instances, we have found that the ink has burned completely through the fabric so that there is now an open-space outline tracing of each letter. The disintegration caused by such a chemical burn is a serious problem to contend with.

We learn from the past to be cautious about what substances we use. It is always best to use safe, inert materials. Over the years, all kinds of crayons and pencils have been tried. Some artists preferred to outline their designs with acrylic paint, and this seems to be acceptable in thin solutions, although we are still uncertain as to the long-term effects. But it seems to be a good medium to work with. It is well to remember that, wherever possible, every procedure should be reversible; that is, you can undo anything that you have done. Reversible procedures are therefore safe procedures. The reason for using a pencil is that many embroiderers feel more secure with a writing technique. Embroidery stitches are always removable, whereas glue, paste, and staples are not recommended because they are not easily removed and they leave a residue.

Once the design has been laid down on the fabric, the fabric should then be put in an embroidery hoop, or the sides of it should be staple-gunned to an artist's stretcher, or frame, of a suitable size. If the work is taut, the stitches will lie flat, the fabric will not bunch up, and the work will not pull in any direction. In order for the work to remain permanently flat, stitches should be made slightly loose since most of the cotton and silk yarns we use today have about a 5 percent shrinkage factor. If you work too tightly, and without a hoop or stretcher, then washing may make the work shrink visibly and distort it.

If the fabric you use needs an edging to finish it off and to keep it from unraveling, I recommend that you stitch a piece of cotton-twill tape to the edges, either by sewing machine or by hand. (Freezer tape and masking tape leave adhesive residues behind them, and again, while we don't know the long-term effect, we do know that glues and adhesives of any kind have very bad long-term and short-term effects on fabrics.) The stitched-on fabric tape can remain on the work all the time, if you choose, if the work is going to be stretched or blocked; or at the discretion of the embroiderer it may be removed when the work is completed.

With the embroidery taut on the hoop or stretcher, the curved needle can come into wonderful play (see Chapter Fourteen on curved needles). Once you have chosen the colors and the stitches that you will use for outlining your design, you may proceed to put them down on your fabric. Do not be afraid to put samples of the stitches you have included outside the main design area of the sampler. It is perfectly appropriate and most charming to do so; letters can be turned into flowers or act as a picture frame in which to enclose a scene. You will notice too that the letters themselves may be decorated around and through their shapes and that the letters can be transformed into other objects, both animate and inanimate.

There is a general lack of quality control in the manufacture of most materials today, even the finest of them, so it is a good idea to check out your materials very carefully before buying and using them. This is especially true for objects that are going to be used anywhere near food or that may need to be washed at some time. Before using a particular fiber, cut a 12-inch (30 cm.) length, wash it, and check it for shrinkage, for dye fastness, or for any change in consistency. Do your own preshrinking. In this way you will feel certain that the embroidered object can be enjoyed and used with pleasure.

28. Hebrew sampler, designed and worked on canvas by Ruth O. Gildesgame, 1976. Author's collection.

3.
EMBROIDERY FOR THE SABBATH

✳ ══ ✳

WHEN WE THINK of embroidering for the Sabbath, we must think in terms of the Sabbath ritual. Generally the table is set with an attractive dinner cloth. I have, in the past, seen all kinds of damask cloths used, as well as embroidered and colored cloths of every variety. I have found in researching the customs of our Jewish forebears, however, that they did not use a large embroidered dinner cloth as we do now. Perhaps they considered that their tablecloths would not fit various sizes of tables, or they may have been included as part of a trousseau. Also, since a tablecloth often gets soiled easily when it covers the complete table, it would have needed laundering after each use. What our forebears did instead, therefore, was to make embroidered table centerpieces.

The Sabbath Table Centerpiece

These table centerpieces were usually round, square, or oblong pieces of fabric, embroidered with various Sabbath scenes or Sabbath prayers. The most beautiful ones came from Eastern places such as Kurdistan, Samarkand, and Bukhara. There are a few of each in the collection of the Jewish Museum in New York and others are in the Israel Museum and the Hechal Shlomo Museum in Jerusalem. The origin of the one from which I worked my Sabbath centerpiece has still not been identified.

30.

In the early 1950s, I obtained a flocked, white-on-white reproduction in nylon of a circular Sabbath cloth measuring approximately 32 inches in diameter. This reproduction (Illustration 29) came from Paris with a little paper identification that said the original cloth was made in the seventeenth century and had included psalms and prayers written on it in Hebrew. The paper also gave French translations of the Hebrew words. I received the cloth as a gift from a friend who said she had acquired a gross of them through a wholesaler; but after sending photographs to museums all over the world, I was still not able to track down the original cloth, which is probably Persian or Bukharan. While many Sabbath cloths are of similar origin and design, no two are alike. After spending many years trying to locate the original, I decided that I would adapt the design from my reproduction onto contemporary fabric, taking much artistic license.

The circular Sabbath cloth, Illustration 30, was made in 1972 from a cotton/polyester blend fabric. The embroidery was done with DMC cotton. Many setbacks were suffered before the project was completed, but a lot was learned about embroidery techniques and problems along the way. The fabric was prepared by washing it first and then stitching a hand-rolled edge all the way around. It was placed on a covered Homasote board, with dressmaker carbon laid over it and the nylon, flocked reproduction placed on top. With a number two pencil, I traced through the nylon reproduction and the carbon paper and onto the cotton fabric. This was both a laborious and a painstaking chore that took two days!

One of the things that I learned at this time was that the pins used for affixing, while they were rustproof, left carbon-paper pinmarks on the fabric that could not be washed out with ease. Another problem was that I had to buy several packages of dressmarker carbon to get enough of the colored papers I wanted in order to provide sufficient contrast against the white cotton. I ended up using a variety of blue, red, and green carbon papers for the actual transfer of the design. It is interesting that the blue and green carbons rubbed off very easily in the process of embroidering, while the red stayed on and would not wash out well for a long time.

I subsequently learned, the hard way, that the cotton floss had a small percentage of shrinkage and that I should have done my embroidery a little more loosely. Somehow we are always afraid that we will embroider too loosely, so we often end up embroidering too tightly.

What is wonderful about the Sabbath cloth is that—while there was a small percentage of shrinkage, and it is now necessary to block this table

Top: 29. Close-up detail of reproduction of a Bukhara Sabbath cloth made in Paris in the early 1950s. Author's collection. Center: 30. Adaptation of Sabbath cloth reproduction (as seen on jacket back), using vibrant cotton-floss embroidery on polyester and cotton ground fabric. (See Color Plate 10.) Made by Ita Aber. Bottom: 31. Detail of Illustration 30.

centerpiece with pins each time it is laundered—it is easily laundered in the washing machine and is therefore used and enjoyed very much.

While working recently with the collection at the Jewish Museum in New York, I found similar cloths and examined them closely. What was interesting was that the embroiderers had used a cotton or silk perle thread that was far more coarse than the fine cotton floss used on my adaptation. As it turned out, my work was finer—and it need not have been. Because I had not seen any of the original centerpieces until after my work was completed, it was difficult to figure out whether the nylon, flocked version was showing the design in positive or negative position. Some of the flowers looked as though they should be reversed. Therefore, in executing the embroidery, each flower was different—which is not the case with the genuine cloths. My centerpiece has turned out to be something of a sampler. I still hope to find the original someday.

Left: 32. Sabbath cloth, Bukhara, nineteenth century. Courtesy of the Moldovan Family Collection.   Right: 33. Persian *chalah* cover, early twentieth century, executed in silver-metal thread and fringe on silk. Author's collection.

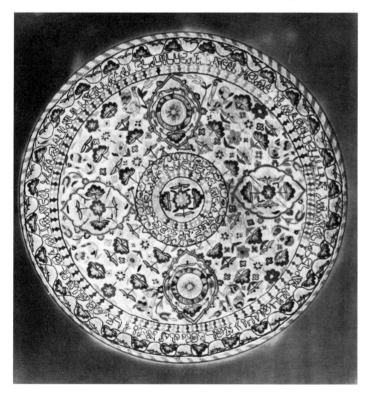

For embroiderers planning to make a Sabbath-cloth centerpiece today, I would recommend that they use some of the antique embroideries as a source of inspiration but that they not try to make an exact copy. Be inspired by the past but don't live in it—make something of your *own* time.

The Sabbath cloth used each week could also include notes of personal family dates and occasions and be highly individual. The idea of putting Sabbath phrases around the edges of the cloth is very attractive. It is also appropriate to include family members' names and perhaps even dates of birth, leaving room to add names over the years. There is no reason why contemporary religious embroideries should not be an expression of our own time while still employing fine-art needlework techniques and customs along with quality materials.

Another object that is very useful and attractive is the Sabbath bread (*chalah*) cover. It is even more fun to have several of them. The reason for this is that if one gets soiled when it is used on Friday evening, another will be available for use on Saturday. People also enjoy having extra ones to give their children and to give as gifts. Also, when one has guests for the weekend, it is always nice to have an extra *chalah* cover for them to use.

The Sabbath Bread Cover

MATERIALS
* Pencil
* Paper
* Graph paper
* Hardanger fabric
* Backing fabric
* Embroidery hoop
* Needles
* Cotton embroidery floss
* Scissors
* Thimble
* Fabric on which to lay down finished embroidery for enlargement

The Sabbath bread cover, Illustration 34, was designed by Tsirl Waletzky and executed by me. We worked it together as one of a limited-edition embroidery. Using the concept of "limited edition," we treated this original work of art as a limited, numbered graphic—which, in fact, it is. The *chalah,* or Sabbath bread, covers were prepared with different colors of yarn, leaving it to the embroiderer to decide on her own stitches and color usages. The idea was to limit the edition to ten so that whoever made such an embroidery would, in fact, have an original signed and numbered work of art not unlike a fine-art print. We believe that embroidery is a fine art—that we are, indeed, painting with a needle. Since we have chosen the needle and thread as our tools for the execution of these works of art, there seemed no reason why they should not be signed and numbered by the artists as original, limited-edition works of art.

34. "Fishbird" *chalah* cover No. 2/10, designed by Tsirl Waletzky and executed in chain stitch and satin stitch on hardanger and laid onto a solid fabric with feather-stitching, Made by Ita Aber.

Illustration 34 is number 2/10 and is signed, on the right, by the designer and, on the left, by the embroiderer. It is entitled "Fishbird." Also shown is a *chalah* cover entitled "Dove of Peace," designed by Tsirl Waletzky and worked by Lavina George Abraham (Illustration 36).

One of the things we discovered in our work was that while we enjoyed using the hardanger fabric for this particular design, we felt that there was not a sufficient amount of fabric to make it as large as we would have liked. Therefore, we appliquéd the design on a larger ground fabric. The appliqué was worked with classic feather-stitching. Please note that the embroidery and the ground fabric were each washed separately before being put together. This object has been washed many, many times; it is very successful and is thoroughly enjoyed.

35. Design for a limited-edition Sabbath *chalah* cover by Tsirl Waletzky.

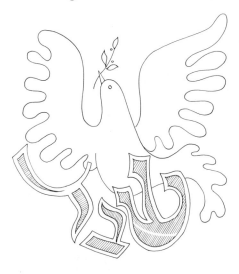

36. "Dove of Peace" *chalah* cover, designed by Tsirl Waletzky in limited edition and executed by Lavina George Abraham, Riverdale, New York.

Other Sabbath Embroidery and Ideas

In addition to table centerpieces and *chalah* covers for the Sabbath, one can make all kinds of embroideries that are used and useful. Among them are skullcaps, in all manner and variety of decoration.

Women's head coverings for the saying of prayers are also appropriate. They can be made from a round piece of fabric, with embroidery added, or from a square or triangular piece, like a kerchief. They may also be a long scarf. Some of the familiar head coverings come from Israel and feature Yemenite embroidery along their edges. Women's head coverings have often been made of lace. Why not make a head covering or scarf of cutwork, hardanger, linen on linen, or silk or cotton embroidery? Floral motifs and prayers for the Sabbath candles are appropriate and very beautiful on them.

37. Designs for men's and women's head coverings.

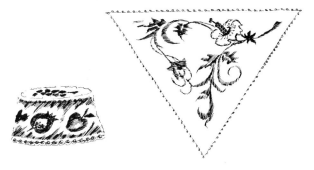

38. Design of grape cluster, depicting the blessing over the wine. In whatever material the design is executed, a good finish would be to couch a gold cord around the grapes.

Bible and prayer-book markers are also excellent gifts and projects for embroidery.

This most unusual and beautiful spice box (Illustration 40) is of fiber filigree; it was made by Ina Golub. The center of the fiber construction has a liner of Plexiglas for holding the spices.

Left: 39. Bible or prayer book markers on grosgrain and velvet ribbon with a heavy glass bead at the bottom. Made by Ita Aber.   Right: 40. Spice box of fiber filigree made of wool and cotton fibers with a Plexiglas insert. (See Color Plate 19.) Made by Ina Golub. Courtesy of Dr. and Mrs. David Brailowsky, Mountainside, New Jersey.

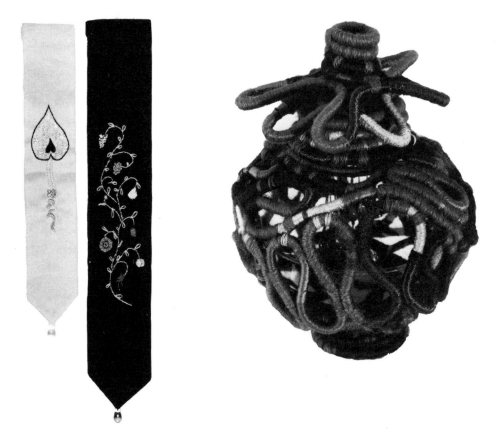

Many Jewish families and groups have different traditions that were handed down to them. Whether Ashkenazic or Sephardic, groups of people from different places have certain added rituals from which ideas can be taken for embroidery. A North African Jewish tradition is that

Left: 41. Bukhara skullcap used for special occasions, early twentieth century. It is made of gold metal threads on silk with a knit border. (See Color Plate 12.) Author's collection.   Right: 42. Two skullcaps from Israel made by Yemenite embroiderers in gold and silver metal threads on white satin. Author's collection.

after a family has said the Friday-evening blessing for the wine, it begins a series of blessings called "*Maya Brachot,*" which means "one hundred blessings."

They commence by making a blessing for the fruit of a tree, then they bless a vegetable from the ground—often a radish, a carrot, or peanuts—then they say a "*Shehakol*" blessing for beer or fish, and then they bless rose water or spices. After all of the aforementioned are performed, they then wash their hands and make the blessing for bread; when they add the salt to the Sabbath bread, they recite, "*Adonai melech, Adonai malach, Adonai yimloch l'olam va'ed.*" Besides being an alliteration, this means "God is King, God was King, God will be King of the universe forever."

Left: 43. Hand-washing towel of linen with silk embroidery, Italy, 1666. Courtesy of the Rothschild-Strauss Collection, Cluny Museum, Paris.   Right: 44. Hand-washing towel, in folk art concept, painted in acrylics on linen with overembroidery of cotton threads. Fully washable. Made by Ita Aber.

The Prayer Shawl

A prayer shawl, or *talit,* is a piece of fabric, generally a square or rectangle, with fringes located at the four corners. It is finished with a decorative band at the top that is called an *atarah,* the Hebrew word for "crown." During prayer , the shawl is brought up around the head so that what we call a neckband becomes a crown. In very orthodox synagogues, people pray with *talitot* on their heads right through the service, not just during some portions of it.

The large prayer shawl shown as Color Plate **7** is made of an eighteenth-century silk brocade finished with gold metallic fabric and woven with tiny red pomegranates and green leaves. Its origin is probably France or Italy.

Spanier arbeit means "Spanish work." It describes a method of wrapping silver- and gold-metal threads over cotton cords in an embroidery and weaving technique. It is used on all forms of ecclesiastical embroidery. Neckbands, such as the one in Illustration **46**, were made in Europe until World War II, and are classic examples of an old art form. These have always been very desirable prayer-shawl decorations.

Many people are making their own prayer shawls and neckband decorations. Dorothy Wolken, of Pittsburgh, is well known for her work using classic ecclesiastical embroidery techniques with silk and metal thread, and employing gold or silver kid leather (or suede) as part of her design.

45. Prayer shawl with neckband made of metal threads in the 1940s by machine. Courtesy of Joshua Aber, Yonkers, New York.

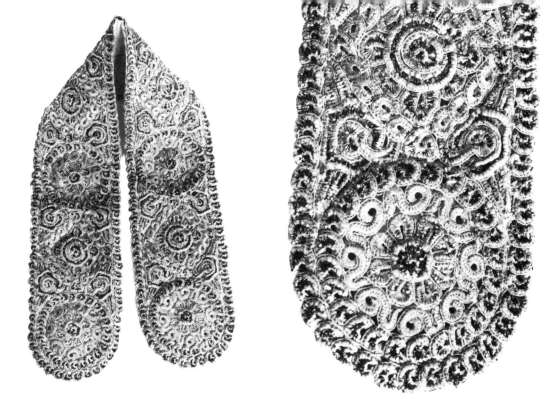

Left: 46. *Spanier arbeit* neckband *atarah* made of silver-metal threads wrapped around cotton cords in a weaving and embroidery technique. Private collection. Right: Detail.

Left: 47. Prayer shawl of silk with a neckband, by Dorothy Wolken. Made of gold kid, with beads and metal threads depicting the word *chai,* it features the hands of the *kohanim,* as the owner is of the priestly tribe. (See Color Plate 6.) Courtesy of Joshua Aber, Yonkers, New York.   Right: 48. Rabbinic stole by Dorothy Wolken depicting the pillars Jachin and Boaz. Made with silk and metal threads, gold wire, braid, and gold kid. Courtesy of Rabbi Aaron B. Ilson, Coconut Creek, Florida.

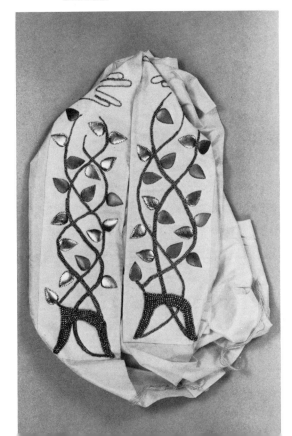
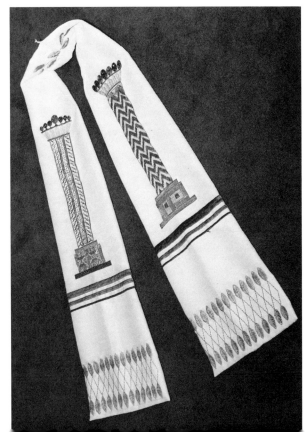

To make the prayer shawl (Illustration 49) for our younger son, I was inspired to use his name, taken from the tribe of Asher, and went to the Bible, Genesis, Chapter 49, to check the quotation from Jacob's blessings to his sons. For the tribe of Asher, he said: "As for Asher his bread (shall be) fat, and he shall yield royal dainties." The Rashi interpretation says that "the produce he shall yield will be in great abundance like olives which will give forth oil like a fountain." (See Color Plate 5.)

To prepare the design, there were several things to consider. One was that the child belongs to the priestly tribe *(kohen),* so that the prayer shawl needed to be large. The larger size was a necessary consideration, since he might join in synagogue worship where he would participate in the blessing of the congregation. Because this is done during the High Holidays, the shawl needed to be very lightweight. A white Dacron and cotton fabric was chosen. The design of the sheaves of wheat was worked with Jacob's blessing surrounding it. The wheat was made of couched Yemenite gold thread with yellow DMC cotton in straight stitches. Jacob's blessing was worked in satin stitch using mauve DMC cotton floss, with the name Asher in contrasting turquoise-blue cotton floss. The priestly hand at the top of the star is a stylized version of the child's own hand, executed in blue and worked in satin stitch.

49. Details of prayer shawl of cotton with appliqué-embroidered neckband shown in full as Color Plate 5. The center of the neckband motif is also worked separately and appliquéd. Made by Ita Aber. Courtesy of Harry Asher Aber, Yonkers, New York.   A. Detail of *talit* showing pomegranates and their blossoms and leaves. B. Detail of hand from *talit* appliqué.   C. Detail of *talit* showing treatment of Hebrew letters.

A

B

The family name at the bottom was fun to do. The Hebrew lettering was inspired by illuminated manuscripts. From right to left, the *aleph* was done in blue satin stitch with a Hebrew flag as a finial for the letter. The *beth*, done in gold satin stitch, is surrounded by mauve grape clusters in French knots, and the *resh* features a dove worked in red satin stitch. The whole was done on a separate six-pointed star-shaped piece of fabric that was then appliquéd to the ground fabric.

The young man for whom the shawl was made was involved in the decision-making process. He selected a fabric that he was comfortable wearing and he helped to work out the size. He also helped select the neckband design of pomegranates (for which pomegranate plants were purchased in order to study the blossoms and the leaves more closely). The neckband was also worked on a separate piece of fabric and then appliquéd. The reason for using the appliqué technique was so that the reverse side of the prayer shawl would be very neat. The finishing was done in gold braid.

The corners of the *talit* were reinforced with squares of fabric, and hand-stitched buttonholes were made to accommodate wool ritual fringes. These were prepared by the young man's father according to the prescribed knotting sequence. (Until *The Jewish Catalog* was published, we had crumply old pieces of paper with the knotting sequence notated on them as a reference.)

C

There are eight wool threads involved. One of them is longer than the rest. This is a three-handed job—one person makes the knots while a second person holds the corner taut:

Make a double knot through the hole in the prayer shawl;
Wrap the long thread around the remaining seven threads seven times, holding the knots very firmly;
Double-knot again;
Wrap eight times;
Double-knot again;
Wrap eleven times;
Double-knot again;
Wrap thirteen times; and
Double-knot again.

If it is done properly, all the threads will be perfectly even when the knotting is completed.

50. A. Cords for the ritual fringes are held perfectly straight, with one cord held longer on one side.   B. A double-hitch knot is made and . . .   C. the longer cord is wrapped seven times around the group of strings. This must be held perfectly taut or the cords will unwind. (Ask another person for help.)   D. Continue the wrapping and knotting as prescribed, until the last wrap-around. The thread that started out longer should now be the same length as the others.

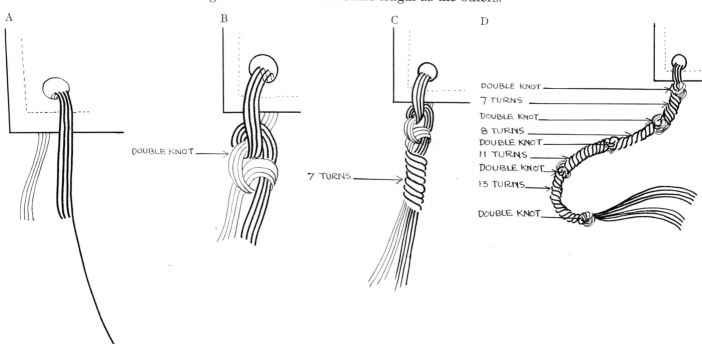

A   B   C   D

DOUBLE KNOT

7 TURNS

DOUBLE KNOT
7 TURNS
DOUBLE KNOT
8 TURNS
DOUBLE KNOT
11 TURNS
DOUBLE KNOT
13 TURNS

DOUBLE KNOT

51.   The ritual fringe should lie smooth. Avoid bunching the fabric.

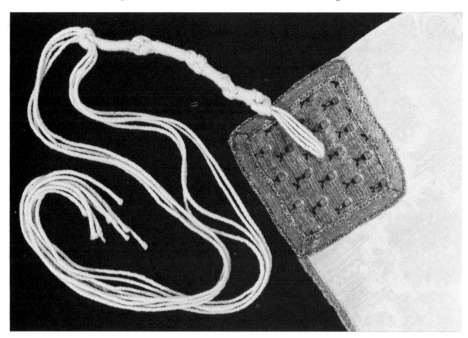

52.   Neckband of silk Indian Parsi embroidery appliquéd to wool *talit*. Braiding of the fringe was made by a restless child twenty years ago and was left that way. Courtesy of Joshua Aber, Yonkers, New York.

4.
PROJECTS
FOR THE
COMMUNITY

✳ ──────────────────────────────── ✳

MANY COMMUNITIES in this country are involved in embroidery projects and are interested in commissioning embroiderers to design or execute works of art for the embellishment of their sanctuaries. These community projects have been handled in many different ways. Sometimes a member of the community who is an artist is asked to design something for the synagogue. There are also local art stores or needlework supply stores that do designing, and they are sometimes asked to create a design to be worked by members of the community. From my experience, many of these efforts turn out to be not very successful. Unfortunately, problems of politics or personality arise, and discord is sometimes created, and I would like to suggest methods to avoid this.

One recommendation is that the persons responsible, in a particular temple, commission a design from a professional artist. This design can then be embroidered by volunteers, the artist who made the design doing the supervision. (The artist might even prefer to designate some local professional embroiderer to supervise the commissioned work.) The community thus acquires an original work of art, designed by a fine artist and supervised by an embroidery professional. No member of the congre-

46.

gation is responsible. This keeps the work running smoothly and generally assures the community a finer work of art.

We know that in Judaism the only thing that is really important is people. Our trappings are always replaceable. Members of the community can always perform the services and other important religious functions. Praying can take place in a private home, and services usually can be led by a person over the age of thirteen.

The large and beautifully designed synagogue was never commonplace in Jewish life until the twentieth century. Today, however, in the Western Hemisphere there are many beautiful temples and synagogues, embellished with sculpture, stained glass, murals, graphics, cast bronze, forged steel, and textiles of every variety. Among the textile furnishings that may be included are: wall hangings (such as appear in Chapter Five), ark curtains of endless variety and made of almost every material, torah mantles to cover the holy scrolls, lectern covers, seat covers, and so on—only our imaginations limiting the possibilities.

The Ark Curtain

Included as Illustrations 53 to 56 are several exceptional ark curtains that have been made by contemporary artists in the United States.

The curtain by Ina Golub (lower left) reads: "Blessed is the Lord daily." It is worked in appliqué and embroidery with couched threads and beads of every variety. The close-up photo shows some of the lovely details of this excellent artist's work.

53. and 54. Ark curtain and detail. Appliqué couched cords and beads by Ina Golub. Courtesy of Temple Beth Ahm, Springfield, New Jersey.

Another exceptional ark covering are the ark doors (Illustration **55**) designed by Amiram Shamir. These canvasworks were done in DMC tapestry yarn on canvas, with white chalk cut beads, and yellow Vaseline-glass beads. The embroideries were worked on two separate panels mounted on doors in the chapel of Salanter-Akiva-Riverdale Academy, Riverdale, New York. The artist permitted me to interpret and execute his design in the manner in which I saw fit. (For those who might be interested, there are 116,000 stitches in this work, which took six months of eight-hour days to complete.) To complement these doors, I designed and made a matching torah mantle.

55. Ark doors designed by Amiram Shamir, embroidered in DMC wool on canvas with beads by Ita Aber, read: "Halleluya." (See Color Plate 14.) Courtesy of the SAR Academy, Riverdale, New York.

56. Ark doors designed and made by Sophia Adler of silk appliqué with classic feather-stitching technique. Courtesy of Bet Torah Synagogue, Mount Kisco, New York.

Another outstanding piece of art work is this ark covering (Illustration 56), located in Mt. Kisco, New York. The artist, Sophia Adler, executed her design in silk appliqué and classic American appliqué tradition, using feather-stitching. She began with a mock-up and rough sketch of the concept. Furthermore she was concerned with the kinds of fabric that were to be used, whether they would wear well and could be easily cleaned; for this she went to several museums for advice.

Many artists are concerned about how one works with a synagogue or community committee. The general consensus is that it can be a difficult task. Several artists have said that while the relationship is usually excellent, sometimes the committee is not sensitive enough to the artist's needs. Many congregations do not think in terms of the usefulness of the objects they are commissioning. Some artists have told me that the artist always thinks of the ark decoration and the Torah (with its mantle) as being the focal points and, therefore, the most meaningful parts of the service. Fine artists should be compensated appropriately for the fine-art objects that they create, but many of them have difficulty charging a

sufficient amount. Unfortunately, some people with little talent charge a lot, and have more talent at public relations than at art. This is not a problem unique to synagogue decoration: it exists everywhere in the art world. What is sad is that several very fine male artist/embroiderers have quit working on synagogue projects simply because they have not been able to make a living at this work. These artists have been forced to work only in the area of secular art.

It must be said, however, that many artists are fortunate and find sensitive, trusting, and sophisticated congregations that are willing to work with them in an open-minded way, showing proper respect for the creative artist.

The great and famous ark curtain shown as Illustration 6 in Chapter One is the work of the European master embroiderer Jacob Koppel Gans. The three-dimensional appliqué work and embroidery are exceptional. It is an outstanding creation, breathtakingly beautiful.

The Torah Mantle

A few outstanding torah mantles also have been worked in recent years. One of these, by Sophia Adler, is entitled "Kaddosh," which means "holy." The covering depicts a candelabrum. It is worked in her classic appliqué technique in bright silk fabrics (Color Plate 2).

I designed and worked a torah mantle (Illustration 57) for the rededication of a holy scroll that had been rescued from the Nazi destruction of a Czechoslovakian community. The scroll had originally been pre-

57. Torah mantle detail commemorating "Kristalnacht" depicts silver heishi as barbed wire that turns into stars. Made by Ita Aber. Courtesy of the Conservative Synagogue Adath Israel, Riverdale, New York.

sented 150 years ago by the parents of a newborn son to their synagogue. The holy scroll and the mantle were rededicated to a synagogue on the anniversary of Kristalnacht, also known as "the night of broken glass." The design symbolizes the talmudic story of Rabbi Hanania ben Tera-dyon, who was burned to death by the Romans in the second century with a holy scroll wrapped around him. As the flames were consuming him, he told his disciples that he saw not the burning of the parchment but the letters of the holy scroll rising to Heaven.

The design depicts the flame and the letters, but it also depicts the barbed wire of the Holocaust. The letters spell out the first and last words of the five Books of Moses—"In the beginning" and "Israel"—rising above the flame and the barbed wire. The mantle itself is made of silk, and the embroidery is executed in silk thread, with the barbed wire made of liquid-silver heishi. Interestingly enough, the grid of the barbed wire is only visible close up; from a distance, the barbs sparkle like stars in the sky. This mantle is located at the Conservative Synagogue Adath Israel in Riverdale, New York.

To make a torah mantle, one first needs a beautiful design and fine choice of materials. But because it is intended for long-term use, there are some special considerations. Will the mantle be used by young people or older people? How often will it be used? What size scroll is it going to fit? It is important to make the design proportionate to the size of the scroll. The top, between the "trees of life," or staves, should be carefully measured. (A piece of one-quarter-inch plywood should be cut from a paper template made especially for that fitting.)

You must decide, too, whether the top of the mantle will have

58. Torah mantle appliqué, executed in assorted silk and metal threads and worked on silk with a linen backing. Inspiration from a painting by Charles Seliger. (See Color Plate 13.) Made by Ita Aber.

square or round edges or a simple cloak effect with no stiffening and an epaulette or collar-like finish at the top. These are important considerations because they determine the way the fabric will fall. If a piece of plywood is to be used, then circular wood tops are needed for finishing off. They can be stained or painted as part of the design.

A further decision has to be made as to where the openings of the mantle should be located for ease of putting the mantle on and taking it off. Some styles require slits on the sides, while others are better with a wraparound overlap in the back. For use by children and older people, a large slit on the side is preferable, for easier maneuverability.

The length of the scroll should be measured to determine the necessary length of the mantle. Measurement should begin at the top of the wood disc that surrounds the top staves and go down to at least below the wood disc at the bottom of the staves. Some people prefer that the bottom staves be covered completely. This is a matter of individual choice and taste. A generous hem should be allowed for at the bottom. Line the mantle with a soft fabric like flannel to cover any rough embroidery edges and protect the parchment.

Many very handsome synagogue projects—especially torah mantles—have been worked in canvaswork embroidery of every variety. I would like to suggest a technique for making them even more handsome. We see in early Judaic embroidery collections that there was rarely a mantle or ark curtain made of one solid piece of fabric. Most of them had inserts of valuable brocades or silk-embroidered fabrics brought from faraway places. Some inserts were fragments taken from bridal dresses or from older holy objects that had worn with time.

I encourage this old yet new idea in synagogue decoration: inserting a very fine piece of small-dimensional embroidery as a "jewel" in the "crown" of the Torah. In other words, make a small, beautifully executed, and even expensive embroidery, and appliqué it to any ground fabric chosen as the basic mantle, or cloak, of the Torah. This appliqué can be removed when the mantle needs cleaning or is worn out and can be easily reapplied to the same mantle or to any other surface. Traditionally, these appliqués were finished off in silk or gold lace, silver braids, and trimmings (used for church and synagogue) of grape clusters and leaves. Some embroiderers today use handmade edgings to finish a work of embroidery.

Left: 59. Torah mantle executed in "fiber filigree," which is a wrapped cord technique. This is worked in multicolored yarns with reds predominating. Made by Ina Golub. Right: 60. Torah mantle in velvet with clear Plexiglas top, embroidered in silk as well as with carnelian beads and pearls. Made by Ita Aber. Courtesy of the ASHAR Academy, Monsey, New York.

61. Torah mantles, all executed in gold on white for Temple Emanu-El in New York, 1978. Made by Ina Golub.

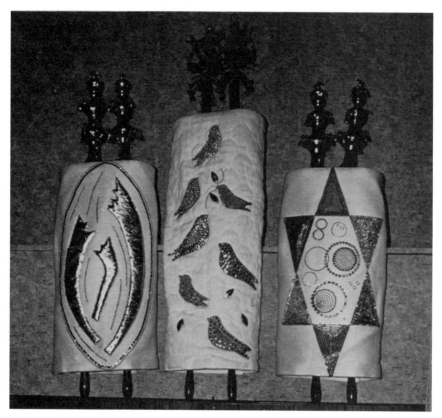

62. Torah mantles, executed in classic ecclesiastical embroidery techniques by Dorothy Wolken. Courtesy of Temple Emanuel, Pittsburgh, Pennsylvania.

63. Cover for a reader's desk, Italy, eighteenth century. The probable maker is Laura, wife of Eliezer Finzi of Recanati. Executed in undyed linen with tan linen embroidery. Courtesy of the Friedman Collection, the Jewish Museum, New York.

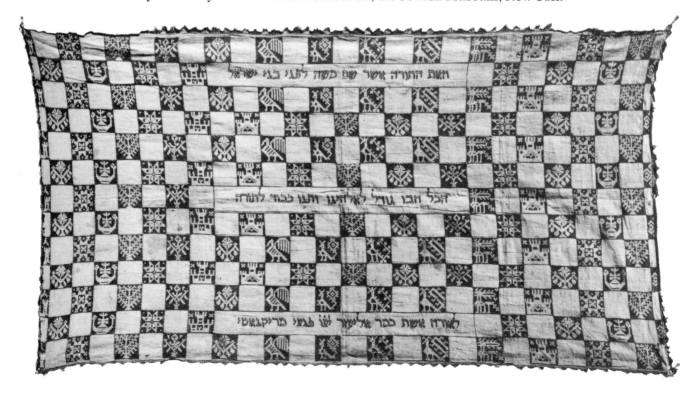

The Torah Breast Shield

MATERIALS
* Paper
* Pencil
* Graph paper
* Muslin
* Embroidery hoop
* Needle
* Thread
* Final material of either linen or silk
* Artist's stretcher
* Linen, silk, or cotton embroidery floss
* Thimble (if the embroiderer uses one)
* Ruler
* Scissors
* Bristol board backing material
* Backing fabric, edging, or ribbon trim
* Metal threads (if they are to be used)

Another idea for individual participation in community projects is the making of embroidered torah breast shields. They can be designed in many ways, but one good way is to honor the birth of a female child. It is appropriate to take design ideas from that portion of the Torah for the week in which the child was born (see Chapter Two). The design can be successfully worked out and embroidered on a surface that can then either be applied to a simple ground fabric or attached with a string around the neck of the scroll (as is generally the case).

While the front of the breast shield may be highly decorated, the reverse might say that it was made in honor of the newborn child, including the date of birth and, if you wish, the name of the embroiderer as well. (The embroiderer may be a parent, grandparent, other relative, or family friend—someone who feels close to the newborn child.)

One reason for making contemporary torah breast shields is that many synagogues find it necessary to have security alarm systems installed on their holy arks. Unlike the silver breast shields, the embroidered torah shield would have little value to a thief. A different torah breast shield can be made for every portion of the Torah that is read for the Sabbath, as well as for holidays.

A torah breast shield is also a lovely presentation gift of a girl to the synagogue for her bat torah or bat mitzvah. She might even execute it herself, using the Torah portion and the day of the week she was born, her zodiac sign, and any other symbols that appeal to her.

When we say *"Mazal tov"* we are wishing a "good constellation." When we sing *"Siman tov"* we are wishing a "good sign." These popular expressions, which stem from an ancient tradition, are seen on antique torah binders, but we don't often think about their meaning or realize what they imply. Check rabbinic sources for more information on the significance of the zodiac symbols.

The first two sketches shown (Illustrations 64 and 65) were inspired by the seven fruit species of the Bible: pomegranates, figs, dates, wheat, barley, grapes, and olives. The first breast shield (Color Plate 11), of pomegranates, was made with genuine garnet beads, mother-of-pearl, and silk and cotton thread on a linen ground. A design was worked out on paper. The original concept was to be executed in a long and narrow style. The design was transferred to linen with a number two pencil, and the fabric was held taut with staples on an artist's stretcher. The materials used were Ver à Soie silk (the dye was set with a saltwater solution), DMC floss, green mother-of-pearl flower petals, genuine garnet beads, wrapped gold cord couched in Belding Corticelli silk, and with gold trimming by the yard. (The project was begun on an airplane trip to London and completed one week later on the return trip.)

Left: 64. Sketch of torah breast shield featuring pomegranates and leaves. (See Color Plate 11.)   Right: 65. Sketch of torah breast shield featuring figs and leaves. (See Color Plate 11.)

The stiffening material was two-ply bristol board. Interestingly enough, the completed shape was originally supposed to be a classic shield form. However, while I worked at a round table to complete the mounting, I suddenly saw it from another angle. I turned it sideways and finished it in the new direction—which proved to be far more appropriate and satisfying.

The second breast shield, featuring figs, was executed in silk appliqué with gold cotton kid and silk embroidery on silk fabric. This was also mounted on two-ply bristol board with a linen backing. The finishing edge is headband material, generally used to finish off the binding of pages in a book.

The third shield in Color Plate 11 was made with Zwicky silk and DMC cotton perle petit point on 32-mesh silk gauze, and includes couched Yemenite gold thread. The ground stitch was done by working "lower left to upper right" but going up four threads and back two. This is an excellent ground-covering stitch, especially when the thread is thin but the color, sheen, and look of the fiber are right. A stitch can always be devised to cover. Please note that there has not been a new stitch invented in many hundreds of years.

The design for this breast shield was inspired by the Megiddo horned altar. This archaeological artifact features four horns, one on each corner of the altar, where the holy tablets were placed. By joining two horns

Left: 66. Israelite horned altar, tenth or ninth century B.C.E., excavated at Megiddo by Professor Yigael Yadin. Courtesy of State of Israel, Ministry of Education and Culture, Department of Antiquities, Jerusalem.   Right: 67. Torah breast shield, made in Morocco of gold-metal thread on velvet, nineteenth century. Courtesy of the Israel Museum, Jerusalem.

Left: 68. Sketch of conjoined horns inspired by the Megiddo altar, depicting a heart-shaped design.   Right: 69. Final design of conjoined horns for torah breast shield. (See Color Plate 11.) Made by Ita Aber.

together, we get a motif that looks like enjoined ram's horns and a design that is heart-shaped. Archaeological excavations have also revealed heart-shaped columns in some of the basilica-style synagogues, including the one excavated at Capernaum. Archaeological designs are excellent.

The Torah Binder

Torah binders have a marvelous history (see Chapter One). There are many kinds. In Italy and the Middle Eastern countries these binders were often made of fine woven materials and then wrapped around the holy scroll to keep it from unrolling. (The name wrapper and binder stated exactly what the object did.) In Italy and France, we have found beautiful embroidered binders, some of which may have been executed by professional embroiderers but certainly by fine, highly skilled artists.

70. A photograph, in sequence, beginning on the right, depicting a torah binder, dated 1809 and executed in silk embroidery on linen. Author's collection.

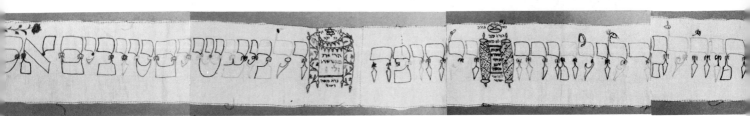

The 1809 binder, Illustration 70, is from the author's collection, and reads, from right to left: "Benjamin, son of Chaim Aryeh ("lion") . . . *sh'lita* ("who shall live the prescribed number of good days allotted to him, amen") . . . was born . . . *b'mazal tov* ("under a good constellation") . . . on the thirteenth day of Teveth 569 of the small date [without the 5000 included]. He shall be beautifully raised up. The Lord will raise him up to Torah, to marriage, and to the performance of good deeds. Amen, Selah."

In order to figure out a date in the Gregorian calendar, add 1240, the year in the Jewish calendar when the Gregorian calendar began. Therefore, 569 plus 1240 equals 1809.

Every Hebrew letter has a numerical value, and in these binders (as in many synagogue embroideries), abbreviated words are used in contracted form. In this binder, as in many Judaic embroideries, words are often made by taking the first letter of several words and contracting these into a smaller word that represents the words that were eliminated. This means that the contraction *bar*, which stands for *ben rav*, means "son." Next there is *sh'lita,* which is the contraction for *sheyiche l'orech yomim tovim amen*, which means "who shall live the prescribed number of good days alloted to him, amen." Next is the date *tof, kof, samech, tet,* which numerical equivalent is 400 plus 100 plus 60 plus 9, totaling 569—followed by *l'pak*, which is the contraction for *lifrat katan*, which means the small calendar date (without the thousands counted). The next contraction is *yatav*, which stands for *yagdil torah v'yaadir*, which means "He shall raise up the Torah and glorify it." Last but not least is *Aleph, Samech,* which stands for "Amen, Selah." Not all torah binders were circumcision cloths. Many were made to honor marriages and special events. Some were made specifically as a torah wrapper.

Many contemporary binders are not dedicated to a male child but rather are designed to mark significant occasions or simply to be beautiful ornaments. Illustration 71 shows a binder by Dorothy Wolken. It was worked in gold kid, beads, and metal thread on blue suede, and lists the five Books of Moses. It has a Velcro closing.

71. Torah binder depicting names of the five Books of Moses, in Hebrew, worked in metal threads and gold beads on blue suede. Made by Dorothy Wolken.

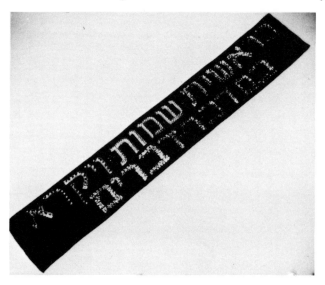

The Marriage Canopy

Marriage canopies have been made by many individuals as well as synagogue groups. (Each house of worship has its own special problems of size and installation.) In years past, canopies were commercially made —generally of white satin—and were not carefully stored. By contrast, the fine handmade designs executed in recent years often are used as wall hangings in the sanctuary when not in use for a marriage.

An example of such a double-duty canopy is seen as Illustration 72. By Fran Willner, it is located at Temple B'nai Abraham in Livingston, New Jersey. It was designed so that the front posts are eight feet high, while the back posts are six feet high. With this slanted installation, the underside of the canopy can be seen easily by the congregation; the underside, here, has the concentration of design.

קול ששון וקול שמחה

72. Marriage canopy made of antique embroidery fragments applied and sheer fabrics laid over each other for graphic effect. It has birdseed sewn on the trunk of the tree, plus rhinestones and beads. The top reads, in Hebrew: "The voice of happiness and the voice of joy." Made by Fran Willner. Courtesy of Temple B'Nai Abraham, Livingston, New Jersey.

Tsirl Waletzky designed the marriage canopy shown as Illustration 73 as a family heirloom. She used paint with appliqué and embroidery on cotton. The wording around the valance edge in Hebrew and in Yiddish may be translated: "The voice of joy and the voice of happiness, the voice of the groom and the voice of the bride." The underside depicts two doves of peace. The canopy was designed with removable, portable poles and can be folded neatly away when not in use.

Recently, some lovely canopies have been made of crewel embroidery, but they are not really an expression of our own times.

73. A marriage canopy of embroidery, paint, and appliqué. The top reads, in Yiddish: "I am my beloved's and my beloved is mine." The side is done in Hebrew. The underside features appliquéd doves. Made by Tsirl Waletzky.

5.
WALL HANGINGS

✳ ══════════════════════════════════════ ✳

Ideas for Temples and Community Centers

Every artist whose medium is embroidery can be inspired by existing sources. By that I mean that inspiration can come from the world that surrounds us, from the objects with which we are familiar, and from the study of places and things that preceded us. The inspiration for Ina Golub's "Portal" series came from the communities that are actually represented in the embroideries. Each community really exists.

The "Jerusalem Portal," Illustration 74, depicts the arch from the Beth-Alpha mosaic floor. Besides the Beth-Alpha floor, included is a scene of the Western Wall in Jerusalem with people praying in front of it. In addition, this representation of the most important city to Jews includes the agricultural community by showing farmland. The Hebrew word *kvutza* is appliquéd at the bottom.

The Prague wall hanging, Illustration 75, features the portal of the Altneuschul Synagogue. This wall hanging also includes a funeral procession depicting members of the burial society as they are often seen on European Judaic funerary glassware. A street scene of Prague and the Hebrew world *kehila* are also included.

The Amsterdam embroidery, Illustration 76, of the "Portal" series features the Toledo (Spain) synagogue, which represents the Sephardic

Top left: 74. "Jerusalem Portal."   Top right: 75. "Prague Portal."   Bottom left: 76. "Amsterdam Portal."   Bottom right: 77. "Krakow Portal." Each of the four wall hangings was designed by Ina Golub and executed by members of North Suburban Beth El Congregation, Highland Park, Illinois. Courtesy of North Suburban Beth El Congregation.

influence in Amsterdam. The scene is of a classic eighteenth-century wedding. It also shows classic row houses, and includes the Hebrew word *minyan*. From Krakow, Poland, the artist selected the portal of a synagogue designed in a classic stonework façade. Hassidim in fur hats are seen studying the law, and the wonderful little wooden village, or *shtetl,* is included along with the Hebrew word *knesseth,* Illustration 77.

Finally, the "Chicago Portal," Illustration 78, incorporates a mixture of many contemporary architectural designs that have been used in North American synagogues and temples. It portrays an interpretation of a harvest festival taking place on the Sabbath. Since each embroidery in the "Portal" series includes a landscape, the American one depicts the landscape of Chicago and features the synagogue in which these embroideries hang. The Hebrew word *aydar,* which means "kin," is also included.

As you will note, each of these wall hangings includes a Hebrew word that refers to the joining together of people in some kind of community. The name of each city has been worked into the arch pediment in English, while the various words that mean "community" have been worked in Hebrew. Each of the wall hangings, therefore, has an arch, a figure group, the English designation of the place, the Hebrew word for "community," as well as a landscape from the place of origin.

The hangings were all made on linen background fabric with appliqué, mixed fibers, and mixed stitchery worked together. Each of the panels measures five feet high by three feet wide. All five are located at the North Suburban Beth-El congregation of Highland Park, Illinois. The project was begun in 1972 by members of the sisterhood, under the artist's supervision, and took three years to complete.

78. "Chicago Portal," designed by Ina Golub. Executed by members of and courtesy of North Suburban Beth El Congregation, Highland Park, Illinois.

Ideas for the Home

Wall hangings are not only for community centers, temples, and synagogues, but may also be decorations for the home.

Sophia Adler's "Menorah" wall hanging depicts a candelabrum, beautifully executed in her wonderful silk appliqué. It is of a size that can grace a temple wall or the wall of a private home.

79. Menorah wall hanging, made of silk appliqué on a woven wool ground. Made by Sophia Adler.

The wall hanging shown as Illustration 82 was inspired by the mosaic floor of the famous Masada fortress (Illustration 80). The design reminds me of—and may have been a forerunner of—rose windows. It also has the quality of yantra, which is a form of mandala (see Carl Jung's *Man and His Symbols*). The uppermost focal window of the Temple Emanu-El on Fifth Avenue in New York City seems to based on this concept, the center of which is a six-pointed star. Earliest human records show these symbols in decorations of many kinds.

80.   Mosaic floor from the Masada excavation, Israel. Reproduced with permission by Professor Yigael Yadin, Jerusalem.

81.   Sketch for wall hanging inspired by the Masada mosaic.

82. Wall hanging inspired by the Masada mosaic floor, executed in wool on canvas. (See Color Plate 18.) Made by Ita Aber.

Widely different groups found meaning in such symbols, all of which seem to be related to the zodiac or the heavens. The design (Illustration 81) of this wall hanging was worked out on a piece of oak tagboard. From then on, the fun began. What looked originally like a terra-cotta color turned out, on closer examination, to be a combination of pinks, blues, mauves, off-whites, brick, beige, and brown.

Having been a needleworker all my life, I worked with three basic stitches and was unaware of the many names being given to the variations. I simply created what was appropriate.

Once the coloring was studied, the technique was quite simple. In order to execute this mosaic pattern it seemed clear that I would execute what were considered to be regular satin stitches in small squares in order to get the effect of little mosaic tiles. This was all done with DMC tapestry yarn.

One decision that needed to be made was whether the design should be squared off all around and/or framed. My final decision to round off one side has always seemed right to me, since only the pattern was important and filling in background stitches to square it off would not have made it more beautiful. (Many years later, when I finally saw the real floor, I was very pleased with my interpretation of it.)

The back of the canvaswork was lined in heavy cotton, and the mounting was done with Velcro.

The only serious mistake was made by the upholsterer, whom I involved in the finishing process. He used ordinary pins during the blocking process, when the embroidery was still wet. This left a rusty pin mark that is permanently visible.

These two renderings for embroidery (Illustrations 83 and 84) were based on the words "In the beginning . . ." They also represent the universe as seen either through a telescope or through a microscope. The microscope reveals a marvelous world of inspiration. While they may appear to be completely secular, they have a religious source and quality for me.

83. Sketch for "In the Beginning . . ." Embroidery inspired by studies in microscopy. (See Color Plate 9.)

For these wall hangings, I cut out round pieces of plywood. The fabrics were mounted on linen and worked in silk and cotton threads. Fiber washers were used for the three-dimensional effects, and I played with detached buttonhole stitches to achieve the varied effects.

84. Left: Sketch for another "In the Beginning . . ." embroidery, inspired by studies in microscopy.   Right: Finished round wall hanging based on sketch. This was executed in three-dimensional embroidery with couched threads and found objects worked on purple silk with a linen backing. The outer edge is finished in amethyst beads. Made by Ita Aber.

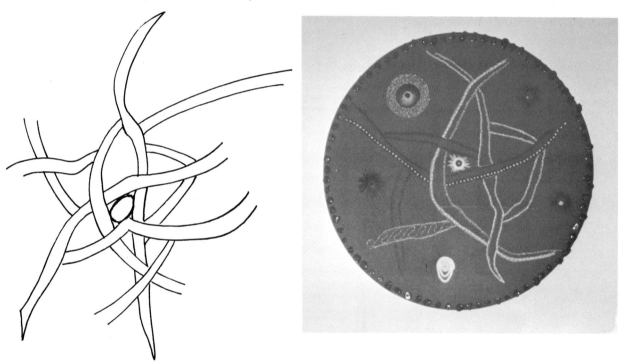

6.
NEEDLEWORK FOR PASSOVER

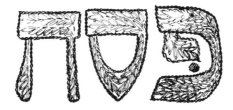

THERE ARE THREE "Pilgrim" festivals in Judaism, so called because it was required that a going-up to Jerusalem be made on foot. The purpose of the pilgrimages was to make a sacrifice, receive priestly blessings, and pay a tithe. The first pilgrimage of the year was for Passover (Pesach); the second was for the Feast of Weeks (Shavuoth, which literally means "weeks"); and the third was for the Harvest Festival, or Feast of the Tabernacles (Sukkoth).

Passover is the biblical New Year, a time of spring planting and of harvesting the winter wheat. Passover is a time for needlework themes of Moses, Joshua, and Aaron the High Priest. The use of the mezuzah is appropriate, as is depicting the parting of the Sea of Reeds.

Moses as an infant in the bulrushes and later as a shepherd leading his flock with staff in hand are symbols of Passover. It is a time for high priests to bless the community at services and for people to bring the winter-wheat tithe to these *kohanim*. It is also a time of census taking. We read of King David with his lyre and of King Solomon, at services. It is also a time for the dedication of the first-born male child to the service of God. (In recent years this ceremony is once again evoking as much interest as it did in the past.)

For home decoration there is, therefore, much symbolism in Passover that can be adapted to embroidery design. On each day of the holiday, different portions of the Bible are read: Exodus, Leviticus, Ezekiel, the Song of Solomon, Book II of Samuel. The counting of the Omer (the barley winter crop) begins. From all of these sources we may take symbols and use them in myriad valid ways.

85. Passover designs adaptable to needlework.

The Passover Pillow

Shown as Illustration 87 is a Passover pillow whose basic design is a crown formed of Jerusalem spring wild flowers. It is to be used by the head of the household to lean on. This pillow—designed by Tsirl Waletzky and interpreted by the author—features papyrus at the lower left and right of the design, below which are waves symbolizing the Sea of Reeds. The X's represent the barbed wire of concentration camps. At the top is a Star of David, made up of the number seven, signifying seven fat years, seven lean years, and seven years of servitude. The materials used were white cotton floss, white cotton perle threads, white surgical silk, and gold metal thread on blue polyester crepe fabric.

86. Passover pillowcase, Germany, late eighteenth century. It is embroidered with rose-silk thread and worked in long-legged cross stitch on undyed linen in the style of Assisi embroidery. Courtesy of the Jewish Museum, New York.

87. Passover pillow designed by Tsirl Waletzky and executed by Ita Aber in white surgical silk, DMC cotton floss, and perle. The phrase written in Hebrew means "All of us are reclining." Author's collection.

The Matzo Bag

A design that can be used for a Passover pillow or a matzo bag is shown (Illustrations 88 and 89) as it looks when laid on a grid for enlarging. Also shown is the enlarged form, ready for embroidery on the fabric.

The lettering was inspired by the old Hebrew illuminated manuscripts and is similar to those seen on old torah binders. From right to left, the letters are as follows: *mem* ("lamb"), *zadik* ("dove"), and *hey* ("crowned lion"). The word *matzo*, while simple in itself, can be made very decorative. It is appropriate to embroider the family surname in the space on the left designated for that purpose or to embroider the name of the needleworker and the date the pillow was made.

Materials suggested are pure linen or all cotton, because these natural fibers have proved to be durable. Since this object will be at the table, located near food, it should be thoroughly washable so that it can be thoroughly enjoyed. Use embroidery linen, and silk or cotton floss (two or three strands) for the embroidery thread. Following are some suggestions for stitches and colors to use for the three letters.

Begin the *mem*—the letter on the far right—at the top of the lamb's head with gold-colored cotton thread, outlining the head and body in tiny stem stitches in order to follow the design's curves. Continue in gold thread, but use satin stitch for the legs of the lamb. The center of each curl has to be a French knot, which may be done in a contrasting color, if you like. Below the hooves is a daisy, to be executed in lazy-daisy stitch in pale mauve with a bright-red cotton satin-stitch center. The foliage at the bottom should be executed in Wedgwood-blue satin stitch.

88. Large sketch for matzo bag.

89. Sketch for matzo bag laid on grid to show method for enlarging designs.

90. Another way of using the same Hebrew lettering, which reads: "Matzo."

The *zadik* dove is done all in satin stitch in Wedgwood blue. Please note that the direction of the stitch indicates the flight of the bird, and gives mood and movement. You may decide that you would rather use split stitches or long-and-short stitches, but remember to keep the feeling of flight. The bird has a lazy-daisy twig in its beak, both made of gold cotton with French knots which may also be done in a contrasting color. The eye is a large French knot worked in red cotton.

91. Illustration of padded satin and illustration of checkerwork with French knots.

The *hey* lion, including the outline of the mane, is worked entirely in small stem stitches. The inside of the mane itself is filled in with satin stitches. It is all worked in gold cotton. The eye is a large French knot made of red cotton, and the crown is worked in satin stitch with three small French knots in red. The leaves at the bottom are in blue satin stitch topped by a flower in gold lazy-daisy stitches and a French knot. The foliated design around the circumference of the embroidery is all satin stitch. The grapes are pale mauve padded satin stitch.

The family name or the name of the embroiderer can be worked of French knots or stem-stitch or split-stitch outline. The checkered design at the top is a stem-stitch outline with a straight-stitch center surrounded by French knots. The checkered design should be done in gold cotton thread, while the French knots can be done in the same gold or in a contrasting color. The rest of the foliage and the name should be done in pale blue cotton embroidery floss. The year may be done in Wedgwood blue. The finishing edge can be lace, gold braid, cotton-bias binding, or any embroidered edge—with or without tassels at the four corners. (Any other material that the embroiderer may see fit and appropriate may also be used.)

In using this design for a Passover pillow or a matzo bag, be sure that you have sufficient fabric allowance for the necessary backing.

92. Matzo bag designed by Tsirl Waletzky and executed by Ita Aber in DMC cotton floss and metal thread on kettle cloth. Finished in gold braid. This object is sponge-cleaned to avoid agitating the gold embroidery while laundering. Author's collection.

93. Matzo bag with tabs. Cotton floss on cotton fabric appliquéd to a larger surface. The buds, in three-dimensional embroidery, were done in padded satin, cup stitch, and needle weaving. Designed by Tsirl Waletzky and Ita Aber and executed in a signed and numbered limited edition. Made by Ita Aber.

If you are making a matzo bag, it should be noted that traditionally three matzoth are used at the seder table, and so three compartments may be added to the bag. These compartments are arranged according to rank. The top one is called Kohen; it was used exclusively by the priestly class. The second one is called Levi, and was for the use of the Levites. The third one is called Yisrael and was used by the rest of the Israelites. A new custom has sprung up where we now add a fourth matzo to represent oppressed Jews everywhere in the world—a reminder that they are never forgotten. This true bread of affliction is called the "matzo of hope." The name of the embroiderer may appear on this fourth compartment.

The second matzo, the Levite one, is also called the *afikomen*. It is divided at the seder and consumed after the meal is finished as a reminder that the Levites were divided. A specially decorated *afikomen* bag, made for this matzo, is another old tradition that has been revived.

A matzo cover, however, can be a single layer of decorated fabric covering the matzoth.

94. Matzo cover that has no compartments. Designed by Tsirl Waletzky and made by Ita Aber in DMC cotton floss and perle. The edge is finished in a running stitch. Author's collection.

The matzo box for the table, Illustration 96, has been made of fabric with cardboard supports stitched into its sides to give it stiffness. While very pretty, it was not launderable. It has also been made in plastic, which does not hold up to wear. I have devised a box made of hardanger fabric and with pockets around the sides to hold Plexiglas supports for the sides and bottom. The corners snap together and open to remove the supports and for laundering by machine (to remove all crumbs and stains). This has been a successful procedure.

95. Matzo box, for the table, as it appears flat. The design "Never Again" is borne out of the concept of *"Zachor,"* which means "Remember."

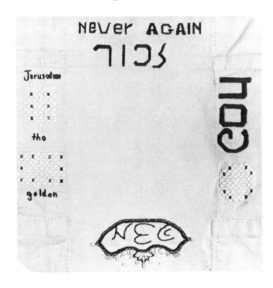

96. The same matzo box, executed in hardanger fabric, has removable Plexiglas sides and bottom. The box snaps together for use at the table. The Plexiglas is removable for laundering. Made by Ita Aber.

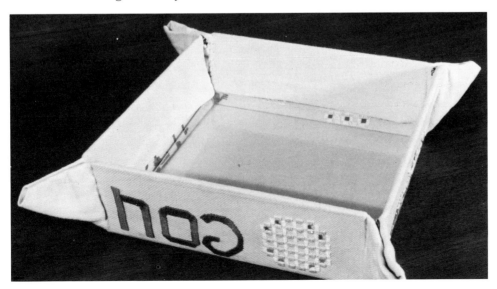

Symbols for Passover Needlework

Passover is celebrated in Nissan, the first month in the Hebrew calendar and the real beginning of the Jewish year. It begins with the blossoming after the winter. It is a spring festival, a time for planting and a time for harvesting the winter crops. The Book of Ezekiel tells us it is a time of resurrection of the dead—a concept of unification of the people of Israel. The egg is used and is a symbol of evolution, death, and rebirth. Other embroidery-adaptable symbols are the flowers of Jerusalem, as well as the trees of Jerusalem, such as the eucalyptus and bokser (carob), with its bokser bread (St. John's bread), well known to Jews on Tu B'Shvat. The traditional Passover motifs of grapes, grape leaves, decanters, glasses, and wine cups can be used for other holidays as well. The drinking of four cups of wine has in recent years been added to; now, in many places, five cups of wine are drunk—the fifth for Israel, to be remembered and blessed. Still other appropriate symbols for Passover are almonds, wheat, bitter herbs (moror), bricks, and matzo—the *lechem oni,* or "bread of poverty," a symbol of poverty—as well as shank bones, apples, walnuts, and lambs.

Sephardic Jews make their haroseth of figs and dates instead of apples, which were traditionally used by the Ashkenazic, or Western European, Jews probably because the exotic Eastern fruits were not available to them. Figs and dates and their leaves are beautiful to use in embroidery. They are, in addition, two of the seven fruit species mentioned in the Bible.

On the second night of Passover, the counting of the Omer begins. Sephardim give out bags of salt. The Omer is a measure of barley (from the winter crop) that was brought to the Temple in Jerusalem; measures of salt were also brought, as it was and still is an important life-supporting mineral. In Judaism, salt is never blessed by itself. Whatever is brought with it is blessed and the salt too receives its blessing by being included.

During the Sabbath service in Passover week, the Song of Songs (Song of Solomon) is read: "I am the rose of Sharon" . . . "the lily of the valley" . . . "the voice of the turtledove is heard in the land." Apples, apple trees, gazelles, and spring flowers are also mentioned, as are singing birds, ripening grape vines, figs, cedars of Lebanon, cyprus trees, pomegranates, frankincense, and myrrh. Spices like spikenard, saffron, calamus, cinnamon, and aloe are specifically mentioned, as are honey and honeycombs.

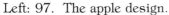

Left: 97. The apple design.   Right: 98. The fig design. Both are adaptable to all kinds of needlework.

The apple (Illustration 97) should be worked in a red satin stitch with a green stem and leaf. The apple blossom should be blush pink with pale green leaves. Use split stitches for the blossom and French knots in the center. Outline the fig (Illustration 98) in celadon-green satin stitch and work the center and the leaf in satin stitch in a darker green. Work the bottom navel in dark-green satin stitch.

The colors that dominate the aforementioned are gold, ivory, yellow beryl (a pale canary-yellow color), tarshish (which is chrysolite and known to us as peridot, a lovely shade of pale apple-green), sapphire (royal blue), lapis lazuli (royal blue with gold flecks), pearl, ruby (red), and amethyst (purple).

Passover symbolism might, rightly, commemorate the establishment of the State of Israel in the year 1948, or 5708. We might also remember, in symbolism, the years 1939 to 1945; and the figure of Srulic, that brash little sabra in short-sleeved white shirt, short blue pants, and work hat—brazen and indestructible.

"Seder" means "order"; we remind ourselves that there is no freedom without law and order.

The Passover Table Covering

For the making of a table covering for Passover, I suggest the following: Because everyone uses different tables and each of us can generally make our own tables larger or smaller, in keeping with classic early Judaic tradition, the tablecloth may be an embroidered centerpiece, which is then laid over any plain tablecloth. It is then not necessary to have embroidered cloths of varying sizes, nor is it necessary to concern ourselves with what size to make or whether the embroidered cloth will fit.

Another one of the advantages of making a centerpiece for the table instead of a tablecloth is that more time and detail can be given to it. It is surely less clumsy to work with, and the commandment from Exodus 26:31 demanding that the embroidery for the Holy of Holies be made with skill and cunning can here be fulfilled. (By the way, Exodus 26 through 28 makes excellent reading for the embroiderer.)

It is generally advisable, before starting on an important project of this type, that the embroiderer buy small quantities of various fabrics with which to experiment. Spill some wine on the sample swatches and try dripping candle wax on them. See how they wash out. See if they shrink. Do the colors run? It is always a good idea to check these fabric properties before beginning a project, so that an appropriate fabric can be safely selected.

The embroidered centerpiece, called a *mappa* in Hebrew, may be round, square, or oblong. It may be of any convenient dimensions. But it should be made of washable materials—linen and cotton are suggested —so that it may be continuously enjoyed.

The following series (Illustration 99, A to G) is instructions for making our table centerpiece.

99. A design, in series (pp. 82–84), for a Passover table centerpiece with a checkerwork center.

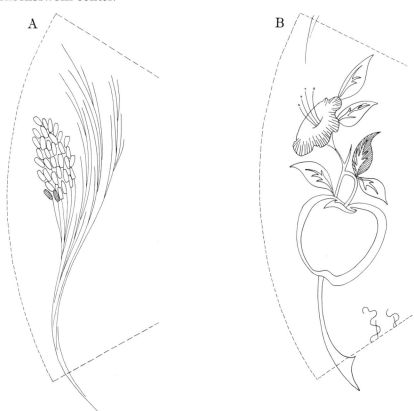

A   B

C

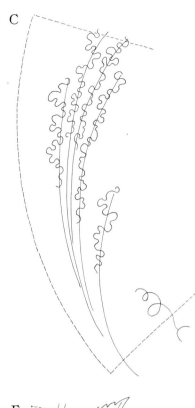

D

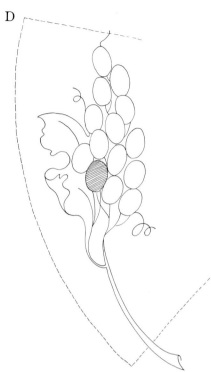

E

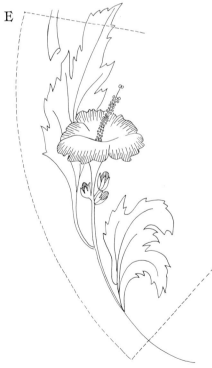

F

G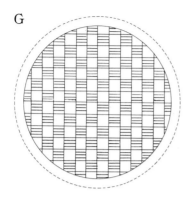

Trace the group of designs, set forth for the table centerpiece, onto a large piece of tissue paper. You will need six pieces for tracing out this design. You will note that the figures in Illustration 99 indicate where the designs should meet. The first illustration has the dates. The dates should be a brownish-gold color worked lengthwise in satin stitch. The stemwork and the palm frond are to be worked in the same shade of leaf-green and should be carried throughout the project. The palm frond should be worked in split stitch and the stemwork also in split stitch. Please note that the stemwork from the dates goes into the next part of the pattern, which is an apple and apple-blossom design.

The apple is to be worked in small stem stitch around the circumference in apple-red. The blossom should be a soft pink worked in long-and-short stitch around the edge. The outline of it should be in split stitch. The stamen should be the same brown-gold as used earlier. The leaves worked in the leaf-green should be satin-stitched around the edges, leaving the center of each leaf showing the ground fabric. The stem should be solid satin stitch.

The stem of the apple goes into the next section, which features bitter herbs. For the bitter herbs I have selected parsley here—although there are other kinds of bitter herbs that are also used at the seder. Work the parsley in leaf-green chain stitch. All its stemwork should be in split stitch.

Following this is a cluster of grapes, to be worked in purple. The grapes should be outlined in split stitch and then filled in with chain stitch. Work the leaves and curls in leaf-green split stitch. The stem is to be done in satin stitch. Please note the join-up to the herb design.

The next part of the design is the rose of Sharon, which is mentioned in the Song of Solomon. It blooms all summer long in North America. Use pink for the blossom, leaf-green for the leaf and stemwork, and brown-gold for the stamen. Split stitch is recommended for the foliage and stemwork. The large blossom itself should be outlined in split stitch, and long-and-short stitches should be used around the edges. Please note that this trumpet-shaped blossom is actually five petals joined together. The buds always appear below the blossom and should be filled in with satin stitch in the same pink. The stamen should be worked in a series of French knots. This is most effective. I include figs here, and though we generally see figs in their dark-colored dried state, these figs are fresh. When they are dried with molasses they are almost black. When they are very ripe they appear purple, but their fresh, edible state is green with reddish striations on the inside. These figs are to be worked in purple in chain stitch. The leaves are to be executed in outlined green split stitch, as is the rest of the foliage. The navels at the bottom of the figs should be done in red satin stitch. Work the main stem in satin stitch, too. It is designed to join the motif in front of it and the motif in back of it.

The checkered center is to be worked in a white checkerboard pattern in straight satin stitch. Work the outline in split stitch. The reason for using the checkered motif in the center is because the Book of Exodus gives specific instructions for the making of checkered designs (see Chapter One).

100. Table centerpiece featuring fruits and vegetables used by both the Sephardic and Ashkenazic communities. Executed in cotton floss and silk thread on white organza. Fully washable. Made by Ita Aber.

The Passover Hand Towel

Early Judaic embroideries remaining to us show lions executed in a checker design of red and white squares. We also see this in Purim and Passover hand towels. Passover towels sometimes show a round matzo done in the checkered design, which almost makes it look like a real handmade matzo. Checker motifs are, therefore, in the early Jewish tradition, and make a good filling pattern for borders of tablecloths and table covers, Passover pillowcases, and a finishing edge for a matzo cover.

Left: 101. Ceremonial towel for the Passover seder. European, circa 1800. Embroidered of red cotton and multicolored silk on undyed linen with a border of knitted, undyed linen lace. Courtesy of the Jewish Museum, New York.   Right: 102. Passover hand towel, eastern European, nineteenth century. Red perle cotton on white cotton ground in classic folk art tradition. Courtesy of Cora Ginsburg.

Plate 1. Torah mantle made from a silk Japanese obi and embroidered in pearls, the design of which is a crown. The style of the mantle is that of a woman's dress, as the Torah is considered female. Made by Ita Aber.

Plate 2. Torah mantle made of silk appliqué worked in the design of a menorah. Made by Sophia Adler.

3.

4.

Plate 3. "Tree of life" executed in appliqué of silk and rayon with antique French glass leaves stitched on. Made by Ita Aber.

Plate 4. Sun wall hanging is paint on linen and is overembroidered with linen couched cords, mirrors, and celluloid gumdrops. Painted by Amiram Shamir and embroidered by Ita Aber.

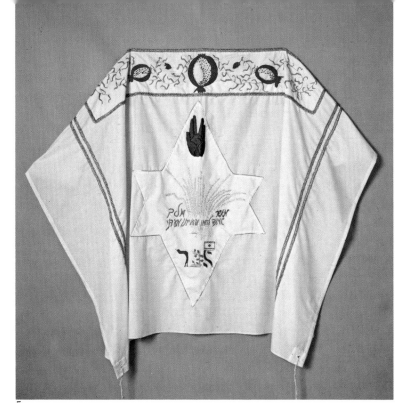

5.

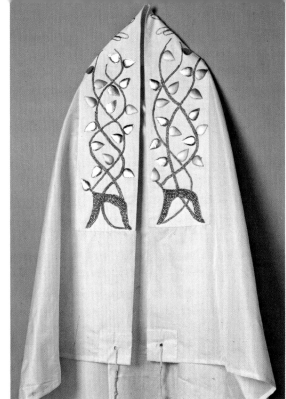

6.

Plate 5. Prayer shawl of appliqué and embroidery features pomegranates for the neckband, an inscription from the Bible using the child's Hebrew name, the hand of the priest, and the family name at the bottom. Made by Ita Aber. Courtesy of Harry Asher Aber.

Plate 6. Prayer shawl of silk worked with gold kid, silk and metal threads, and beads. It features the hands of the *kohanim* at the neck, because the owner is of the priestly tribe. Made by Dorothy Wolken. Courtesy of Joshua Aber.

Plate 7. Prayer shawl from the eighteenth century of silk brocade with red silk pomegranates embroidered on gold lamé appliquéd to the neckband and the four corners. The country of origin is either Italy or France. Courtesy of Joshua Aber.

7.

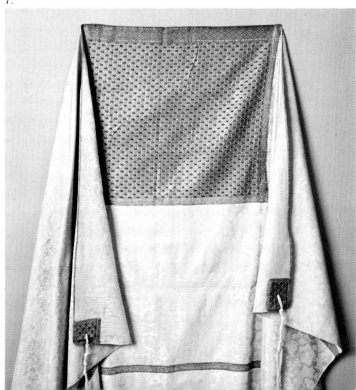

8.

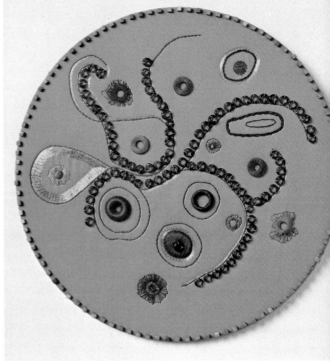

9.

Plate 8. Piano bench cover executed in DMC cotton floss on petit point canvas. It features an assortment of symbols including a labyrinth from the *Kabbalah,* three fish, and the priestly hand. Made by Ita Aber.

Plate 9. Wall hanging entitled "In the Beginning . . ." worked with mixed fibers, "found" objects, dyed bone beads. It is inspired by a view through a microscope. Made by Ita Aber.

Plate 10. Sabbath table centerpiece adapted from an antique Bukhara Sabbath centerpiece. Executed in cotton floss on cotton polyester and featuring psalms and Sabbath blessings around the edges of the design. Made by Ita Aber.

10.

12.

11.

Plate 11. Top left: Torah breast shield depicting one of the seven species of vegetation — the fig — executed in silk appliqué with metal and silk threads. The edging is of book headband material. Bottom left: Torah breast shield inspired by the Megiddo horned altar executed in silk, cotton perle, and Yemenite gold thread on a thirty-two silk mesh canvas. The bells of brass have clappers. Right: Torah breast shield made of silk and metal threads, using garnet beads for the pomegranates and green mother-of-pearl for the leaves. It is worked on linen. Made by Ita Aber.

Plate 12. Left: Russian skullcap executed in petit point canvaswork, soft structure. Right: Bukhara skullcap made of silk- and metal-thread embroidery over a stiff crown, with a knit border and a single feather trim. Acquired in Israel. Author's collection.

Plate 13. Torah mantle appliqué worked in silk and metal threads. It is inspired by the work of the artist Charles Seliger and was made by Ita Aber.

13.

14.

Plate 14. Ark doors designed by Amiram Shamir made of DMC wool and old glass beads by Ita Aber are shown set in the ellipse ark and surrounding stained glass. Courtesy of SAR Academy, Riverdale, New York.

Plate 15. Mezuzah cover made of gold-painted wood Victorian beads and worked on canvas. This door parchment cover has a pocket at the back for the parchment and a recessed hanger. The center beads are red-dyed bone and white ceramic. Made by Ita Aber.

15.

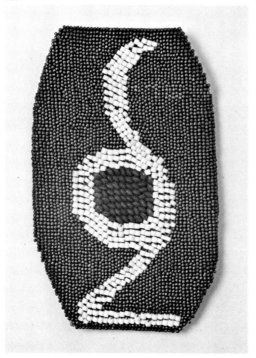

16.

Plate 16. Left: Sabbath bread cover executed in limited edition on hardanger fabric appliquéd with feather-stitching on woven fabric surface. Right: Matzo bag for Passover made of appliqué and cotton embroidery. The pale blue area in the design of a six-pointed star is all worked in split stitch with the flowers and buds overembroidered. Both were designed by Tsirl Waletzky and executed by Ita Aber in limited editions.

Plate 17. Samplers of Hebrew lettering. The one worked on canvas (left) and the other on muslin (right) give some ideas for Hebrew lettering design. Made by Ita Aber.

17.

18.   19.

Plate 18.   Wall hanging executed in DMC wool on canvas featuring the Masada mosaic floor excavated in Israel. Made by Ita Aber.

Plate 19.   Spice box by Ina Golub made of fiber filigree in a cord wrapping and stitching technique. Courtesy of Dr. and Mrs. David Brailowsky.

Plate 20.   Passover pillow made of polyester crepe and embroidered with surgical silk and cotton floss and perle. The star at the top is made up of the letter "7"; the bottom includes papyrus as well as barbed wire and waves. Designed by Tsirl Waletzky and made by Ita Aber.

20.

You can also make a simple linen hand towel in cross stitch for the hand washing that takes place at the seder. A seder hand towel is appropriate because there are two occasions during the service when all assembled at the table may wash their hands. A bowl and pitcher are generally provided for this and a hand towel as well. The hand towel, of course, should be completely washable. We show here the word *rachtza* ("to wash"). This design can be enlarged and placed at the center of the towel so that either end may be used for hand wiping. You can work the design with a stem-stitch outline, filled with satin stitches, and topped with

103. Passover hand towel to which the Hebrew word *rachatz* (wash) was added. This hand towel started out as a cross-stitch project for a young girl. Author's collection.

104. Left: The word *rachtza* is ideal for adaptation to a hand-washing towel. Center: The design for a wine cup coaster can double as a place card for guests. Right: A bookmark for the Passover *Haggadah* makes a wonderful favor or gift.

French knots. The colors should be very bright—red or blue is very effective. The symbol of the hand, mentioned earlier, is particularly appropriate for a towel. The hand design may be worked around the edges in satin stitch in either red or blue. Embroider the bells, too, in satin stitch. French knots may be used for the bells' clappers.

You may want to use the natural colors of the objects depicted in your embroidery, or choose other colors. The design may even be worked all in one color, as well as all in one stitch. Single-stitch embroidery is in the classic tradition of fine embroiderers, going back to the earliest-known embroidery fragments. Monochrome (single-color) embroidery is also from the finest early-embroidery traditions, both secular and religious. It is often found in folk designs from the Middle East, including classic Jewish folk art.

While the apple and the fig shown earlier were in small dimension, these may be enlarged. They may be successfully adapted for the design of table coasters or whatever the imagination will allow. To enlarge, I suggest that the embroiderer trace the design onto a piece of tissue paper or tracing paper. Depending on the desired final size, you may need several pieces of graph paper for enlarging the design.

After you have drawn the design onto the tracing paper, take a ruler and pencil and mark off a grid over the design. Be sure that you draw squares of equal dimension over the design. You may decide, for example, that a half-inch of the small design will be equal to two inches of the enlargement you wish to execute. Any other ratio of enlargement will work equally well, of course.

Transfer the original design onto the graph paper as illustrated on page 75. The boxes on the graph paper will be helpful in keeping the design in proportion. Finally, trace the enlarged design onto the fabric as instructed elsewhere in this book (see page 25).

Sprays of buds can be adapted for Passover napkin decorations. The colors of the buds may be of your choice, but the foliage should be in leaf-green. Split stitch for the outlines is recommended. The heavy buds themselves can be filled in with satin stitch. Any colors can be used by the embroiderer, but generally bright colors for the buds and several shades of leaf-green for the leaves are appropriate and attractive. Again, it should be emphasized that all the materials should be easily washable. The cotton floss should be of fine quality and it should be used in two or three strands worked loosely—for projects intended for table use.

The Passover Wall Hanging

Joseph's coat of many stripes, *ketonet passim,* is a traditional symbol that is particularly appropriate for a Passover wall hanging.

In our own era, we remember the Holocaust and the striped garb— the modern "*passim*"—of the concentration-camp victims. We have re-membered the bitterness and poverty of the distant past in our Judaic embroidery; it is now a time for remembering the very recent past. Just as bricks and mortar are important symbols, so now the stripes of the concentration-camp garb and barbed wire are powerful symbols. Addi-tional Passover wall-hanging symbols are the open hand in supplication and the clenched fist. Twentieth-century Jews will remember the not-to-be-forgotten yellow six-pointed star patch, with the letter *J* on it, as well as "*Zachor!*" ("Never forget"). Other possible symbols for a wall hanging are: consuming flames that become living leaf forms, rising from the ashes into doves of peace; and the salvia, or sage plant, a symbol of salva-tion. The use of the hand of God is also a symbol of salvation, as is the hand that becomes dove-like in form. The long-tailed turtledove, devoted to its mate and young, is a symbol of peace, harmony, and tranquility— the dove of peace.

105. Butterfly and barbed wire are suggested as motifs for a concentration camp commemorative in needlework.

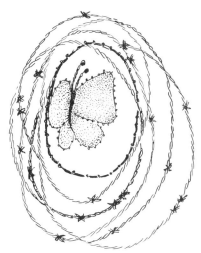

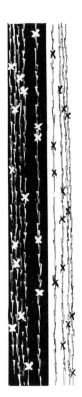

If you decide, therefore, to make a Passover wall hanging, you may want to include such appropriate symbols of the Holocaust as barbed wire and a hand. The wire should be executed in dark gray or black in long stem stitches, in lines $\frac{1}{4}$ inch apart. Up to now, all thread has been used in either two or three strands, but for this design four or more strands should be used to give the heavy quality of the wire. The barbs are made by using regular or long-legged cross stitches—also dark gray or black—across the stem-stitch lines at strategic points.

106. Stripes and barbs, which can be adapted for a hand-washing towel or for a wall hanging as a home decoration, or as a *hamsa* talisman, embroidered with real bells.

107. Barbed wire and hand adapted for a round wall hanging. The barbs are made of small beads in black and white. The hanging is hand-embroidered in black floss with brass bells applied. All work on oyster linen ground. Made by Ita Aber. Courtesy of Tsirl Waletzky.

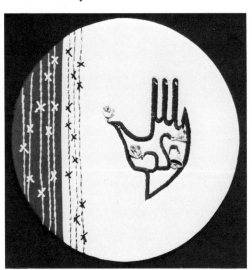

You can make a decorative hanging from wool felt or silk, with appliqué, objets trouvés, or many other combinations of compatible materials. A hand may be enlarged and cut out of felt; it may feature four real bells or some bright beads which would symbolize the four cups of wine drunk at the seder. The colors should be very bright. The bird form, mentioned earlier, symbolizes peace, as does the hand of God that is ever-present.

You may want to add family names and dates or family and Passover symbols to the embroidery. It should certainly bear the embroiderer's name. (See Chapters Two and Eleven.)

This wall hanging need not be washable. However, consideration should be given to its being able to be dry cleaned or, at the very least, vacuumed.

Some Additional Ideas for Passover

Some families use a seder plate for each person at the table, while some Sephardic families pass the seder plate over the heads of all those assembled at the table. In Morocco and western Algeria, the eighth day of Passover is called the Maimona Festival. On this day the people go from house to house and deliver half a head of lettuce, some honey, milk, and fish—all in prescribed measures—as well as five gold coins, in the hope that God will bless them with prosperity. This festival is taken either as a memorial tribute to Maimonides or as *"Yaanenu Hashem"* ("The Lord will answer us").

In many Ashkenazic homes, a white kittel, similar to a short caftan, is worn by men at the seder, while Sephardic men wear a black djelabba and a large heavy-knit skullcap. The Jews from Bukhara use large, heavily embroidered skullcaps as well.

Sephardim, when they recline, have a staff or walking stick by their side so that they are ready to leave for Israel at a moment's notice. Kurdish Jews throw green vegetables at each other to express their good wishes for prosperity in the coming year. The B'nai Israel of India use only dates in their haroseth and make fresh rice chapaties each day. Ashkenazim seldom use rice at all.

Some further objects you might want to embroider for use at Passover include: runners, tablecloths, pillowcases, head coverings for both men and women, skullcaps, wineglass coasters and holders for wine bottles—and anything else that your imagination will suggest. Another suggestion—and a lovely gift—is a ribbon bookmark for use with the Haggadah. The name of the person to whom it is presented may be embroidered in. The design shown as Illustration 104 is outlined with stem stitches and filled in with satin stitches. French knots are used on the six-pointed star. Any colored embroidery floss with beads may be used to finish off the bottom.

All materials used to make Passover embroideries should be sensible and practical. Since they are all used around food, they should be easily laundered and not able to hide crumbs too easily from one year to the next. Pure cotton, cotton and Dacron, and linen fabrics with good-quality silk, linen, or cotton embroidery thread are the most durable and practical.

This is not the time for wool embroidery, like crewel, nor for silk or metal-thread needlework, which are so marvelous for synagogue decoration. It is also not the place for canvaswork embroidery or silk or cotton petit point. These, too, may be used successfully for synagogue decoration or for home use where food does not present an immediate hazard to the needlework. In these instances we concern ourselves only with soot, air pollution, handling, and carelessness—which are problems enough.

7.
SHAVUOTH

THE FEAST OF WEEKS—Shavuoth, or Pentecost—takes place forty-nine days after Passover. (Shavuoth means "weeks"; the word Pentecost comes from the word "fifty," as Shavuoth begins on the fiftieth day.) In Hebrew the word for "week" is the same as the word for the number seven. The Shavuoth feast is celebrated seven times seven days after the celebration of the Passover holiday.

Early sources tell that Shavuoth's character was chiefly that of a harvest festival. A specific ritual in the Temple in Jerusalem was the offering of two loaves—a connection with the wheat harvest. After frankincense had been burned, the two loaves were shared by the priests. Beginning with the Feast of Weeks and until the Festival of Tabernacles, the first fruits of the seven species were brought to the Temple; many, no doubt, brought their first fruits at the same time they made their pilgrimage.

108. Assorted leafy designs, appropriate for almost any occasion.

Shavuoth is a part of the Judaic agricultural trilogy, therefore, and one of the three pilgrim festivals. But rather than being a home festival, like Passover, it is a community event commemorating the giving of the Ten Commandments on Mt. Sinai. It is an appropriate time for decorations to be made for the torah scroll, and many presentations at services are made at this time. Mantles, breast shields, lectern covers, crowns, and pointers presented to synagogues and temples are the order of the day. To commemorate the two-day Shavuoth celebration, people send flowers to each other and cut fresh green leaves to be brought indoors to decorate the interiors of their homes.

Adaptable decorations can very successfully be inspired by the seven species of vegetation mentioned in the Bible—barley, wheat, olives, figs, pomegranates, dates, and grapes. Some temples commission special ark curtains for each of the important holidays, and often the curtain for Shavuoth depicts wheat and fresh flowers—summer is coming.

8.
SUKKOTH AND SIMCHAT TORAH

✳ ══════════════════════════════ ✳

SUKKOTH IS the harvest festival, or Feast of the Tabernacles, while Shavuoth, a spring festival, features blossoms from fruit trees. Sukkoth is the third of the pilgrim holidays, the last agricultural festival.

Many families in the Jewish community build harvest huts and eat their meals there. Many temples and synagogues also make a large harvest hut, called a "sukkah," in which the community enjoys meals together. One of the best parts of this holiday is the decorating of the sukkah with fresh fruits, vegetables, gourds, berries, and grains of every variety. Indian corn is a favorite in North America, as are strings of cranberries.

Pictures, in embroidery, are often hung in the sukkah as decoration. These show examples of the first fruits that are harvested, including grains, squash, and gourds. Many people create a wall hanging with an inscription that reads: "May the Lord raise up for us the falling house of David." Another blessing that is used is the *shehecheyanu:* "Blessed is the Lord our God, King of the Universe, who gave us life, raised us up and brought us to this time." Depictions of the heavenly Jerusalem are embroidered and framed to beautify the sukkah. According to Rabbi Marc D. Angel's book *The Jews of Rhodes,* the community there created elaborately

Left: 109. Citron, or *etrog* plant with classical citrus leaves. From seeds of a single fruit many plants can be grown. The leaves themselves are an inspiration for embroidery. Photograph by Eve Kessler.   Right: 110. Velvet-covered box for *etrog,* embroidered and made in Israel. The inscription reads: "And you took unto yourselves the fruit of the *hadar* tree . . ." Courtesy of Harry Asher Aber.

decorated sukkahs and hung embroidered pictures inside. Items made of paper or non-dye-fast fabrics and yarns invariably get caught in the rain, as the leaf-covered roof of the hut protects nothing inside. It is therefore strongly recommended that all embroideries for the sukkah be in washable and dye-fast materials. If they are also backed with a piece of muslin, this gives them added protection.

Pictures of people gathering wheat, as in the fields of Boaz, are often hung in sukkahs as well.

The palm frond and citron, *lulav* and *etrog* in Hebrew, are symbols of the covenant between God and Abraham and are used during Sukkoth. The palm frond has a woven holder, usually made of a piece of the frond, which holds branches of willow and myrtle. An ornamental box is generally made for the citron. This is sometimes made of silver, but it is often a box covered in embroidery showing the palm frond and citron. A case—very long and narrow—carries the *lulav* to morning temple services during the week of Sukkoth. On the Sabbath of that week, the frond and citron are not used.

It is also fitting, for Sukkoth, to have a table centerpiece showing the first fruits of the season with the appropriate blessings included.

The eight-day harvest festival of Sukkoth ends with Simchat Torah, which is the celebration of the completion of the reading of the holy scroll in its one-year cycle. For this last of the Holy Days the whole community participates in marching around the synagogue with the holy scrolls all dressed up in their finery, every member of the congregation getting a turn carrying the scrolls.

Children also actively participate, and are often given small and even miniature scroll replicas to carry. For these minatures, small torah mantles are made, either in canvaswork or embroidery. These mantles become family heirlooms to be passed along to the next generation. The children carry flags and banners often made of painted or embroidered fabric. It is traditional to put an apple on top of the flag and a candle in the apple, lit for the marching ceremony. Street singing and dancing usually follow up this celebration.

111. Flag from an Israel Day parade signed by then-mayor John Lindsay and embroidered with the New York City skyline. It is used for Simchat Torah processions in synagogue. The reverse side has a big red apple appliqué. Author's collection.

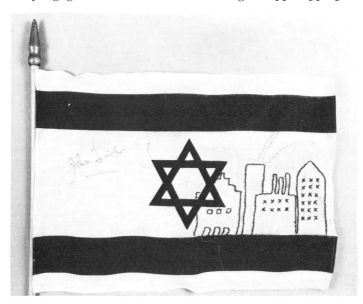

112. Italian embroidery, eighteenth century, part of an ark curtain used for Sukkoth and Simchat Torah holidays. It refers to the prayer for water. Courtesy of the Rothschild-Strauss Collection, Cluny Museum, Paris.

113. Simchat Beth Hashoeva depicts the water-drawing ceremony. Worked in silk- and metal-thread embroidery of the late eighteenth century. Courtesy of the Cooper-Hewitt Museum, the Smithsonian Institution's National Museum of Design.

Simchat Beth Hashoeva occurs on the last day of Sukkoth. In the Temple in Jerusalem people used to watch a water-drawing ceremony. Simchat Beth Hashoeva is the day that precedes Hoshana Rabah, which is the day preceding Shmini Atzeret, the day preceding Simchat Torah.

9.
ROSH HASHANAH AND YOM KIPPUR

✴ ════════════════════════════════════ ✴

THERE ARE MANY interpretations of what Rosh Hashanah, the New Year, represents. Some rabbinic sources feel that it is the agricultural new year, while others contend that it is the religious new year because that was when Ezra the scribe first read the Book of the Laws to the people. We do accept it as the beginning of the new year when the Book of Life is opened and the names of the completely righteous are inscribed therein. We know that the wicked are completely eliminated and the average strive and hope to be inscribed in the Book of Life for the coming year. The holiday of Rosh Hashanah is followed ten days later by the Day of Atonement, Yom Kippur, when the Book of Life is closed and sealed for the year.

When Rosh Hashanah does not occur on the Sabbath, the *shofar,* or ram's horn, is blown in a particular sequence. Members of the congregation are called upon to perform this duty, which requires talent and practice, as the ram's horn is a difficult instrument to play.

The Shofar Bag

MATERIALS
* Pencil
* Graph paper
* Canvas or velvet fabric
* Needles
* Embroidery thread
* Scissors
* Thimble
* *The Comprehensive Hebrew Calendar,* by Arthur Spier (see Bibliography)

The bag shown as Illustration 114 was made of upholstery velvet with a ram's horn design worked on it in DMC floss. The leather carrying-strap, designed to be worn over the shoulder, is from a worn set of phylacteries. Because it's intended for a religious purpose, it is permissible to use worn phylactery leather in this carrying case.

114. *Shofar* bag made of upholstery velvet and embroidered in cotton floss, featuring a ram's horn, which is a suitable symbol. The carrying strap is from a worn set of phylacteries. Made by Ita Aber.

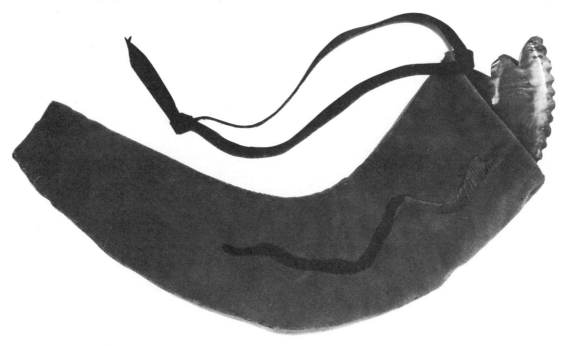

The Prayer Shawl Bag

For the High Holy Days all kinds of ritual objects can be embellished with embroidery: prayer shawls, bags for prayer shawls, skullcaps, women's head coverings, and various decorations for the interiors of Jewish houses of worship. Of the prayer shawl bags shown here, the first (Illustration 115) was made twenty-four years ago with Bernat Tourneau wool on canvas. It has held up very successfully over many years of use.

At the time the bag was made, my husband was still my fiancé. For both of us it was very meaningful to write the word "Zion" on the bag in bold, highly stylized, contemporary Hebrew lettering. In those days there was hardly any blank canvas available, and sources of inspiration, as well as lettering guides, were virtually nonexistent.

When making the bag, I inserted a gusset in the bottom to give it more width. It never looked right and finally, years ago, I removed the gusset, put in a fresh lining of white cotton duck, and couched the top with a red cord to add a little brightness—making it red, white, and blue. Fortunately I had left sufficiently generous seams and working edges all around so that there was no fear of loss of size through unraveling. The quality of the wool and canvas used was excellent. It has held up beautifully and should continue to do so for many years to come.

115. Prayer shawl bag in blue-and-white canvaswork has the owner's Hebrew name and birth date. Made by Ita Aber in 1954 with Bernat Tourneau wool yarn. Courtesy of Joshua Aber, Yonkers, New York.

116. Printed velvet prayer shawl bag overembroidered with genuine coral beads and silk threads. Made by Ita Aber. Courtesy of Jerry Schellenberg.

To make a bag for a prayer shawl, I recommend that you consider the person for whom it is being made. Because so many men carry their own prayer shawl to services with them, it is advisable that their name be put on it. You may choose to work on canvas, or on velvet, or any other interesting fabric.

I suggest that you take the English date of birth of the person for whom the prayer shawl bag is to be made and check *The Comprehensive Hebrew Calendar* for the Hebrew date of birth. Put the Hebrew name and date of birth on graph paper. (Check Chapter Eleven of this book for styles of Hebrew lettering that are suitable.) One side of the bag could have the name and birth date of the person to whom this bag will belong. The other side might include all kinds of other information, like the sampler idea again. A diagram or cartoon of the user's profession or work, and color ideas and design suggestions from the portion of the Torah read during the week when the person was born, may be included. You might also include the name of the portion of the Torah that was read for their Confirmation. These designs make the prayer shawl bag highly personal.

You will note that among the prayer shawl bags included in this section is one on which there is no personal detail whatever. It was made for someone who was not well known to me, but who selected the printed velvet himself, and I set about decorating it. It is highly unlikely that there would be found in any synagogue two such prayer shawl bags; therefore, it was really not necessary to add more personal detail than initials.

10.
PURIM

PURIM TAKES PLACE toward the end of winter, thirty days before Passover, and commemorates the overthrowing of the wicked Haman and the recognition of religious freedom for the Jews by King Ahasuerus of Persia. It is a joyous time, when children dress up in costumes depicting the characters in the story recounted in the Book of Esther.

Adults often participate in masked balls at this time to raise money for charity. For this purpose we are showing three ball masks.

The first mask shown is made of silver lamé. The fabric has a silk warp and a silver-thread weft. The pattern was first worked up in muslin for proportion, style, and size. Doodles on paper, with notations, gave an approximate idea of what the mask would be like. The lamé was laid on linen; both were then staple-gunned to an artist's stretcher and worked together.

On the left of the mask are two Hebrew words worked in early-nineteenth-century French rhinestones, which, translated, mean "And it was in the days of . . ." This is a direct quotation from the beginning of the Book of Esther. The reason for using a quotation was that unless the mask was designated as a Judaic mask, it could be considered quite secular. Under the letters is some red Ver à Soie (silk) thread, couched to draw attention to the subtlety of the wording, which might otherwise not be very noticeable.

The cut-out eyes were finished in black floss worked in blanket stitch to look like heavy eyelashes.

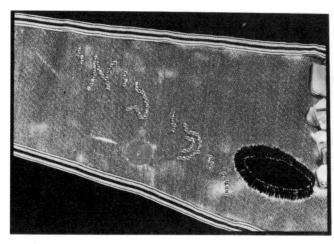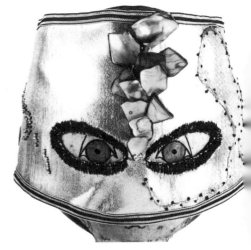

117. Purim ball mask of silver lamé, with antique French rhinestones and silk embroidery thread along with couched Yemenite gold thread. The Hebrew inscription on the left reads: *"Va'yehi bimay,"* meaning, "And it was in the days . . ." Made by Ita Aber.

On the right side is a free-form design worked in Yemenite gold thread couched with gold silk. Red silk French knots accent, as does a black mouche done in DMC floss. Between the eyes are green pieces of mother-of-pearl that have holes and are stitched against each other in overlay pattern.

The edges of the mask are finished in the black-and-gold trimming generally used for ecclesiastical embroidery, which was purchased in England. The closing at the back is Velcro.

118. Purim ball mask, three-cornered shape of gold lamé trimmed in purple silk and French glass leaves. Made by Ita Aber.

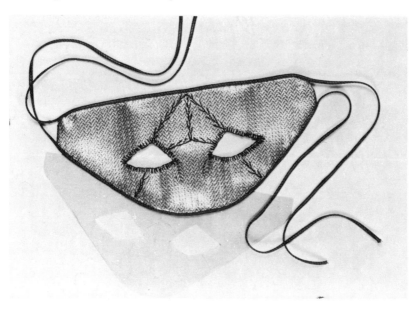

The second mask has a three-cornered design reminiscent of the hat that Haman wore. It is made of gold lamé which has a gold-metal warp and weft and is reversible. The pattern was made of paper, from which a piece of muslin was cut (later used as the lining for the mask), with the eye cut-outs reflecting the same three-cornered shape.

The purple silk floss was embroidered along the edge, and was worked in feather-stitching. Two teardrops of green glass leaves are old French glass. The finishing material was a thin, purple elastic, stitched (in its unstretched state) around the mask, the ties stretchable to fit any size head.

Costumes of any kind can be worn on Purim. In Israel anything goes, with huge street celebrations and performers entertaining at almost every street corner.

119. Purim ball mask executed in purple Japanese silk, embroidered with pearls and gold beads. Designed to fit over the head. Made by Ita Aber.

The Purim Mask

To make your mask I recommend the following: Pick up the Book of Esther in English translation and read through it or a portion of it that may be of interest to you and inspire a concept, an idea, or an image. Make some notations for yourself as to what you think would be appropriate for your mask. Write some of these ideas down and do some drawings on your white paper. When you have the feeling for what you want done, it is then recommended that you lay the design out on the graph paper. (The reason for using graph paper is so that both halves of the mask will be the same size. It is easier to count boxes and that way to keep the mask even on both sides. The design, of course, may be symmetrical or asymmetrical, as the embroiderer chooses.)

Once the design has been worked to proper proportions on the graph paper, transfer it onto the muslin, using transfer techniques previously mentioned. The muslin will serve two purposes: It can be fitted to the wearer and adjusted for perfect fit; it can then also act as a trial material on which to experiment with the design and stitches, and/or it can be used as the lining of the mask itself. Once you are satisfied with the way the muslin fits and looks, transfer the design onto the finished fabric. As mentioned earlier, it is advisable to work the finished fabric through either a piece of muslin or a piece of linen, both of which should be staple-gunned to an artist's stretcher or an embroidery frame. This keeps the work neat and even. The embroiderer can work with ease and can then, when the work is completed, remove the embroidery from the frame and cut it out to the finished size.

At this point, the completing of the mask may begin. Turn in the edges at the back and stitch in a lining as a finish material. This can be the trial muslin or a fresh piece of fabric. Any edgings, braids, or trims may now be added and the fasteners for holding it on the head may also be affixed at this time. (Note that these general instructions are designed to aid and to encourage you to use your own imagination.)

The Purim Hand Towel

There is a feast which takes place in the afternoon of the day of Purim. For this purpose a hand towel is used at the table so that celebrants may wash their hands. Checker motifs, again, are seen at this time, worked generally in red thread on white linen or cotton and depicting scenes from the Book of Esther.

120. Checkerwork hand towel of eastern European origin, used for Purim, Passover, and Sabbath. Courtesy of Cora Ginsburg.

11.
ALPHABETS
FOR
EMBROIDERY

✻ ════════════════════════════════════ ✻

THIS CHAPTER WILL consist of Hebrew alphabets to be adapted for embroidery, plus examples of decorated embroidered letters.

It is recommended that the embroiderer examine a copy of *How the Hebrew Language Grew*, by Edward Horowitz; *The Alphabet of Creation*, by Ben Shahn; and *The Art of Hebrew Lettering*, by L. F. Toby. It is also suggested that the embroiderer peruse the *Catalogue of the Jewish Museum, London; Hebrew Illuminated Manuscripts;* and the catalogue of the Jewish Museum in New York, entitled, "Fabric of Jewish Life." All of these are inspirational sources for the study of Hebrew lettering, its styles and usages in embroidery and decoration. All of these books and catalogues are included in the Bibliography.

While working with English alphabets, I had an unexpected and very beneficial experience. I was sitting at a round table, on which a book of English art nouveau alphabets lay open. I suddenly viewed the alphabet upside down, and detected a few Hebrew letters, which were really upside-down English ones. With the help of the five or six Hebrew-appearing letters, an entire alphabet was constructed. This alphabet design works well for some styles and can be developed from others.

121. Hebrew alphabet in a "straight line" design. Three different-sized enlarge-
ments are also shown for adaptation.

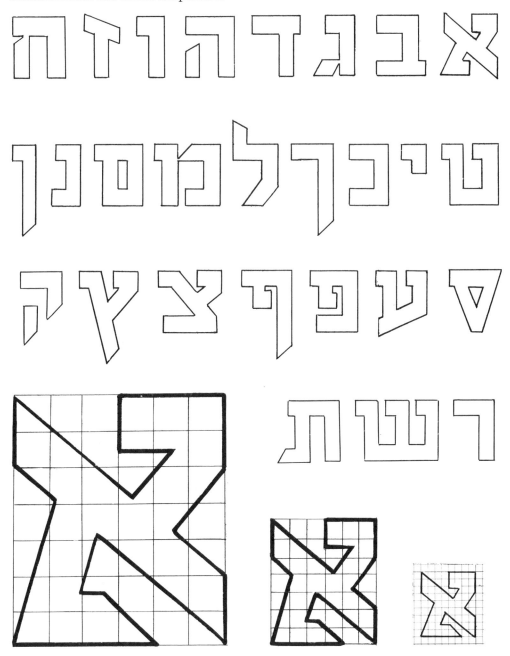

122. Hebrew alphabet in "sharp" style. This may be adapted to canvas or embroidery.

123. Hebrew alphabet in "classic" style. This may be adapted to canvas or embroidery.

124. Hebrew alphabet in "art nouveau" style. This adapts beautifully to embroidery.

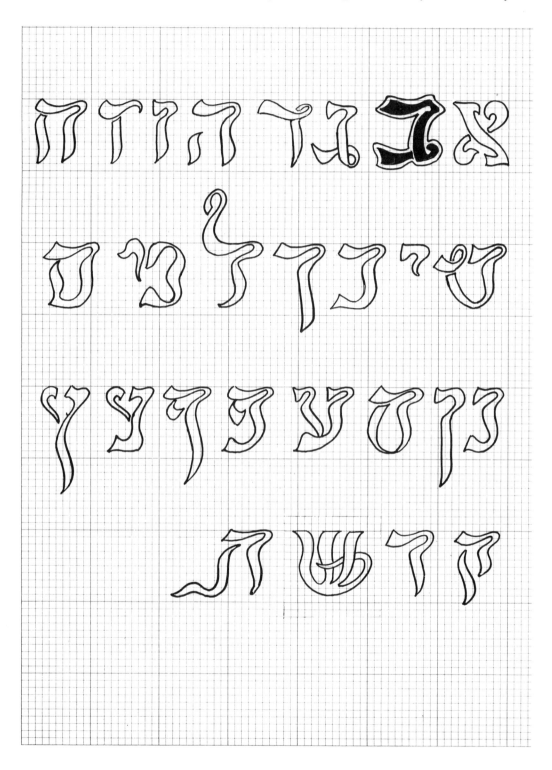

125. Hebrew alphabet in "flower" style. This is classic and very good for home festival embroidery decorations.

126. Hebrew alphabet in "script" style. This is excellent for embroideries of informal design.

127. English alphabet in "hebraic" style. This may be adapted to places where the Hebrew alphabet and usage may not be understood.

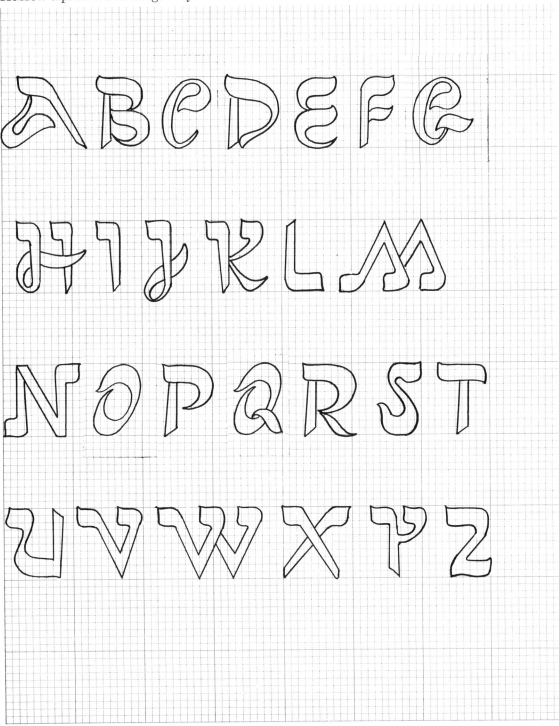

128. Hebrew "straight line" letters worked on a canvas grid for adaptation to canvaswork and counted-thread embroidery.

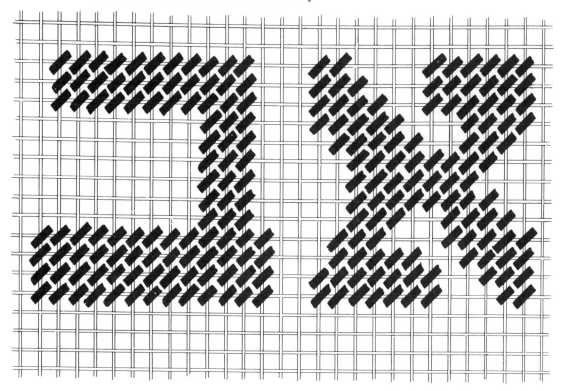

12.
CHANUKAH

FOR CHANUKAH, also called the Festival of Lights, there is mostly a lot of lighting of candles, eating of potato pancakes and doughnuts, singing, money giving, and playing of games.

For Chanukah, as for many other festival days, it is appropriate to have decorated tablecloths or centerpieces. It is also appropriate to have festive skullcaps, and even a festive apron or other personal decorated clothing. We suggest for the home that a wall hanging could be prepared that includes the symbols of the holiday of Chanukah. Because this holiday commemorates the miracle whereby a small cruet of oil—meant to burn for one day—in fact burned for eight days in the Temple of Jerusalem, it is called the Festival of Lights. Sometimes it is referred to as the Miracle of Lights, and the lighting of the Chanukah menorah is a long-standing tradition in Jewish homes. In the Sephardic tradition, only the head of the house lights a "chanukiah." However, sometimes in Ashkenazic homes, for each member of the family there is a separate Chanukah menorah that is lit. Children often make them in school out of clay or pottery and bring them home for use on the holiday. Sometimes the chanukiah, or menorah, is lit with candles and sometimes with oil; many menorahs are made to accommodate both. (The eating of potato pancakes and doughnuts comes about because they are fried in oil.)

The playing of dreidel is another interesting holiday activity. The dreidel is a four-sided top, each side of which has a Hebrew letter that

117.

129. Chanukah dreidel by Diana Grossman. It is made of canvaswork. The construction is copyrighted. Author's collection.

means "a great miracle happened here." Children and sometimes adults play the dreidel, and gamble with pennies—generally for charity. Diana Grossman has designed and made a Chanukah dreidel, or four-sided top (Illustration 129), of canvaswork embroidery. I show this clever and innovative idea, but am not permitted to show how it is made since the design is copyrighted.

The Chanukah Wall Hanging

Symbols such as oil and candles and potato pancakes and Chanukah menorahs are all part of the objects that can be utilized and stylized in a wall hanging.

My choice was to take a candle concept and show it burning. The idea was highly stylized and highly personal. The embroiderer may choose to do a wall hanging that includes favorite symbols of the holiday and this can be hung in the home during the eight days of Chanukah. My choice of material was blue cotton and I then laid out my pattern with a running-stitch needle-and-thread technique. As I worked, the wall hanging made its own demands, and I added gold cotton leatherette as well as all kinds of interesting "found" objects and beads, combined with cotton, silk, and linen threads of every variety. The wall hanging turned out very festive and very bright and, to me, appropriate for the Festival of Lights.

130. Chanukah wall hanging of blue cotton fabric ground worked with gold cotton kid leather and assorted embroidery threads. Made by Ita Aber.

13.
EMBROIDERY FOR THE HOME

✳ ══════════════════════════════════ ✳

We often look for projects for young people to make. "Peacock Body Decoration" is one of them. Two others follow, on pages 121 and 122.

Peacock Body Decoration

MATERIALS
* Paper
* Pencil
* Yemenite gold
* Red linen thread
* Lurex thread
* Aida or hardanger fabric
* Cardboard
* Eyelet punch
* Silk thread

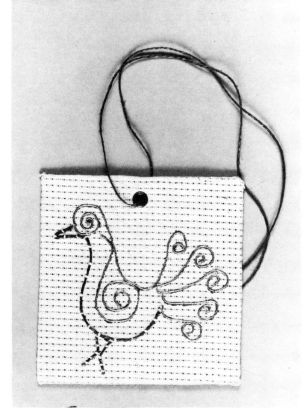

131. Peacock body ornament of couched Yemenite gold thread on Aida cloth with Lurex and linen fibers.

This peacock body decoration is made of Yemenite gold thread, couched in gold silk. The red linen is couched in white and Lurex thread and worked on aida cloth. It was glued to a piece of cardboard, and an eyelet punch was used to make a hole at the top for a red linen string to be brought through for wearing around the neck.

Clothing Patches

MATERIALS
* Paper
* Pencil
* Graph paper
* Canvas
* Assorted fibers
* Needle

Patches for the clothing of young people are popular. This amulet patch features a bird which becomes a hand with an eye in the center—to ward off evil spirits. This is taken from Middle Eastern amulet concepts. It was worked in DMC tapestry yarn on number ten canvas.

Left: 132. Amulet patch made of wool on canvas with *hamsa* talisman.   Right: 133. Dove neckband or bookmark made of Veloura on canvas with glass beads and ribbon ties.

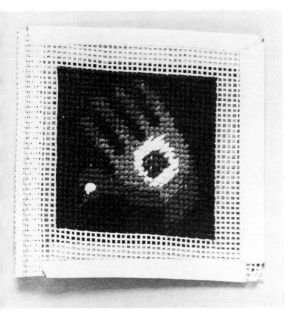

Dove Neckband or Bookmark

MATERIALS
* Paper
* Pencil
* Graph paper
* Canvas
* DMC tapestry yarn
* Veloura fiber
* Persian yarn
* Ribbon
* Beads

The dove neckband or bookmark was worked in Veloura, Persian, and DMC tapestry yarn. It was lined with blue velvet ribbon and finished in green glass teardrop beads and red ribbon ties.

To use as a bookmark, you may turn the embroidery lengthwise and fasten the ribbon and beads to the bottom so they will extend beyond the edge of the book. You can even cut the ribbon into several lengths and add a bead to the bottom of each length, creating a bookmark that is playful.

Mezuzah

The doorpost of a Jewish home usually has a parchment held in a case affixed to it. The doorpost in Hebrew is called a mezuzah. This is reminiscent of the days in Egypt when the Jews were advised to pour the blood of a lamb on their doorposts. Such a sign notified the Angel of Death that these were Jewish homes, so that the angel would "pass over," and the first-born male child would not be smitten. These parchments are set into cases made of silver, copper, ceramic, brass, textiles, and other materials.

134. Two Moroccan mezuzah holders. The one at the left has the family name, while the one at the right has the classic Hebrew inscription to protect the entranceways to houses and rooms. Courtesy of the Israel Museum, Jerusalem.

Moroccan Jews cover their simple velvet parchment holders with beautiful embroidery. They all have "*Shadai*" on them—an abbreviation for "*Shomer Delatot Yisrael,*" which, translated from the Hebrew, means "Guardian of the Doors of Israel." With usage, these three letters, Sh/D/Y, came to signify the name of God. In addition, Moroccans often include the embroiderer's name. Also in classic Moroccan tradition, birds are included in the design.

Top: 135. Mezuzah cover, Morocco, nineteenth century, with a Hebrew inscription. Courtesy of the Israel Museum, Jerusalem.   Bottom: 136. Two mezuzah covers, Morocco, twentieth century. They feature stylized birds in the classic Moroccan tradition. Courtesy of the Israel Museum, Jerusalem.

The contemporary mezuzah pocket shown as Illustration 138 was made of beadwork on canvas. The inspiration for this design came from the excavated synagogue of Beth Alpha in Israel. (Professor Yigael Yadin has kindly permitted me to include it.) The entranceway is a flat, rectangular area that moves into the round form of the constellations and the zodiac and then reaches up to the covenant with God and the Heavenly Jerusalem. This modern design, inspired by an archaeological source, is a way of interpreting such meaningful concepts into our own contemporary terms.

137. This mosaic floor of Beth Alpha Synagogue in Israel inspired a wall mezuzah holder. An entranceway leads a person through the circle of the zodiac signs and seasons through the heavenly Jerusalem. By permission of Professor Yigael Yadin, Jerusalem.

The mezuzah pocket shown was made of antique Victorian gold wood beads for the background, while the design itself was made of red-dyed bone beads and white ceramic beads. Bright brass beads spell the word "Sh/D/Y."

138. Mezuzah holder, canvaswork of gold Victorian beads, painted bone beads, and opaque beads. The word *shadai* (at upper right) is in brass beads. The back is lined with linen and a linen pocket holds the parchment. Made by Ita Aber.

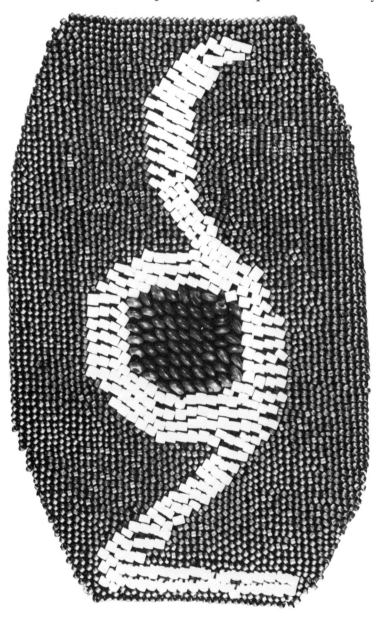

139. This bar-mitzvah invitation designed by Amiram Shamir reads: *"Asher,"* which is the boy's name. The design on the prayer book at the right was executed in colored leather appliqué. Courtesy of Harry Asher Aber.

140. Southern Moroccan woman's headdress, worn during festivals and on special occasions. It is made of silver thread over horsehair with sideburns of pure wool. Early twentieth century. Courtesy of the Israel Museum, Jerusalem.

Bridal Adornment and Pearls

Brides, traditionally, have been beautifully adorned. In some Eastern Jewish cultures, the bride wore her dowry to the wedding as part of her marriage clothing. In the Moroccan Jewish tradition, brides were adorned with jewels, baubles, and amulets as seen in Illustration 141. It appears in the picture here that the bride can hardly move. In our modern times, brides of Moroccan Jewish families borrow such clothing for the wedding, and it is still considered very precious to them.

Left 141. Moroccan Jewish bride, exotically dressed with embroideries and jewels. Courtesy of the Israel Museum, Jerusalem.   Right: 142. Yemenite Jewish brides often wore their dowry to the wedding. The bride pictured is wearing silver baubles and jewels. Courtesy of the Israel Museum, Jerusalem.

The Jewish bride of Eastern Europe generally wore a blouse and skirt to her wedding. Often this was the only new clothing of quality that she owned. These clothes were worn by her on the Sabbath and for special events. A *Brusttuke,* or breastplate, of *Spanier arbeit* was sometimes worn as well. This was a length of silver or gold embroidery that tucked under the collar of her blouse and tied around the neck. The bottom of it would be tucked into the top of her skirt. This was truly a breast shield or ornament, and certainly had a jewel-like quality.

143. Three Jewish brides. On the left is a Yemenite bridal outfit, which includes twenty finger rings and numerous strands of beads. The bride in the middle is wearing a Bukharan outfit, which includes a metallic crown and veil with stars of David embroidered on it. The bride on the right is wearing a Moroccan headdress, which includes artificial black braids and a gold-metal-thread-embroidered short-sleeved jacket with an embroidered stole. From the Jewish Wedding exhibition, Yeshiva University Museum, New York.

The tradition of a white bridal dress is an idea of the twentieth century, both in secular and religious circles. We have, however, been decorating bridal dresses with pearls for a long time. Years ago it was a common thing for me to decorate my friends' wedding dresses and crowns with pearls. I did my own as well.

In the past, when women's skirts or dresses wore out, or could no longer fit, the fabric was cut up and the good portions were used for synagogue decoration. Pieces of the dress or skirt would be incorporated into an ark curtain or a torah mantle, so that these beautiful embroideries or brocades could continue to be used. With time, these were decorated with jewels and pearls. It gave women great pleasure to have them used for religious purposes.

Distinctive head coverings did not emerge until the seventeenth century in Europe, but these too were adorned with ribbons and with glass baubles, which, in time, changed to pearls and jewels. The headdress evolved in the nineteenth century to the *Sterntichel,* and the work of adorning it was highly specialized. Pearls were strung on a wire that was tacked to this head adornment by an expert craftsman known as a *Perlhefter* or *Perlsticker*—which also gave rise to such family names. (Jacob Koppel Gans, mentioned earlier in this book, was a *Perlsticker* of renown.)

144. Bride's wedding crown and veil featuring pearl embroidery. The hat for the matron of honor is mohair, for a summer wedding. Made by Ita Aber, 1954.

Embroiderers who worked in gold were also called goldstickers, and this too was a highly regarded craft. They are known to have worked at the great courts of Europe and to have been employed by the church for vestment decoration. It seemed appropriate, therefore, that I should commission someone—Audry Vinarub—to make a bridal veil for our collection. This fine embroiderer decided to do pulled work on white organdy and created a row of narcissus (Illustration 145). This blossom was selected because it is the real lily of the valley, according to biblical interpretation. The band that holds this circular veil in place is simple; however, a second row of raised blossoms individually made was applied to the veil itself.

Top: 145. Bride's veil of white organza designed by Ita Aber. Executed in pulled-work embroidery and applied individual flowers by Audry Vinarub. The design is of narcissus, alleged to be the real lily of the Song of Solomon; it is also the Rose of Sharon. Author's collection.   Bottom: 146. Detail of Illustration 145, showing a close-up of the blossoms.

In the Sephardic, or Eastern, Jewish communities the Torah was always dressed as a female. In the Italian Jewish tradition the Torah was dressed in a cloak, often with epaulets, certainly of beautiful embroidered brocaded fabrics in magnificent silks. It seems appropriate, therefore, that the Torah referred to the bride; and we know this to be true because, on certain holidays, when a man is called up to the reading of the Torah, he is called the groom. The tradition gave rise to the idea of doing pearl embroidery on a torah mantle, which to me seemed highly appropriate. The concept of a cloak with collar or of a dress is often seen in synagogue use, and it does seem fitting to be included in this section on brides and pearls (see Color Plate 1).

147. Detail of work in progress on the pearl-embroidered torah mantle shown in full in Color Plate 1.

14. CURVED NEEDLES

THE CURVED NEEDLE has been used in embroidery off and on for many centuries. We know that the Yemenite embroiderers of old used them for their work, and that when they came to Israel they continued to use the curved needles until they were either lost or destroyed. Because they could not find replacements, they began to use the straight needle that we are so familiar with. (In the past, these needles were probably forged by hand and made to order, possibly from silversmiths.)

The curved needle, familiar to us for carpet repairs, is generally available as part of a package of assorted needles that are used for upholstery and similar work. The carpet needle has a heavy, squared back and a tapered shaft. The kind of needle that we use is taken directly from surgical supplies and adapted to our needs. A surgical manufacturer in England is producing custom-made ones for me.

A curved needle has been in use for many years by textile conservators and restorers. It made good sense to them, as it does to us, that in repairing the damage on a large textile, if the piece lies flat on a surface, one may use the needle to go over the warp and between the wefts to do the proper restoration without moving the textile in any way. The idea is to manipulate the needle to the fabric and not the fabric to the needle. With a straight needle, one always has to manipulate the fabric—which can cause many imperfections in stitching.

It seemed logical to me, several years ago, that this needle—curved as it is—could be very adaptable to embroidery techniques. There are many different varieties of surgical needles. The ones I was interested in

148. This series of photographs shows how the curved needle should be used for embroidery on fabric and on canvas for right- and left-handed persons.

A. Begin by holding the curved needle between thumb and index finger, using the middle finger as a pusher and manipulator. Learn by using your non-dominant hand and do several rows of running stitches.

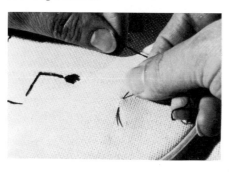

C. Another method of tying down the beginning of a thread is to do a few running stitches in the direction opposite from the direction in which you want to work.

E. To begin working on the canvas, note the position of the needle in the right hand, and that the left hand is always used to manipulate the thread. Try to prevent your finger at the back of the canvas from poking the needle through.

G. Pull it out with the thumb and index finger and manipulate the needle with the third finger into a circle. This turns the needle all the way around; you are now ready for the next stitch.

B. Make a small x to tie down the tail of the thread before proceeding to do a series of back stitches.

D. Go back over the running start stitches to cover them up, and proceed with your work. You will note that there is no tail of thread visible on either the front or back of the work.

F. Push the needle through with the index finger. You will note that the needle must come out automatically from a taut surface.

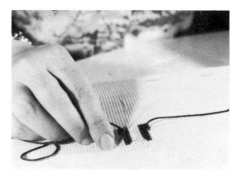

H. The same procedure using the left hand. Push the back of the needle with the left hand. After about fifteen minutes of practice with the non-dominant hand, the embroiderer may switch to the usual hand.

were sharp ones, the intestinal-surgery variety, and dull-tipped ones, the kidney-surgery variety. The sharp ones I use for embroidering through a tightly woven surface such as silk- and metal-thread work, crewel embroidery, cotton and linen embroidery, and for couching threads. The dull-tipped needle is obviously used for canvaswork and counted-thread embroidery, including hardanger, blackwork, and even-weave embroideries that use a count-thread technique.

Needless to say, a fabric surface to be embroidered should always be on either an embroidery hoop, a stretcher, or a frame. The benefits of the curved needle are manifold, not the least of which is that a single stitch is generally achieved in a single motion. The curved needle is not held as any other needle is held. It is held sideways and functions by a wrist action. It is a needle that can be held with any two digits of the hand and it is used in a scooping motion. The embroiderer may still use standing frames or clip-on frames for comfort and pleasure. You need work only from the surface of the work, and since only one hand is used for the actual stitch, the second hand should be used for the manipulation of the thread.

Because this needle is not used or held as any other, I find that when I am teaching its use to someone who does any kind of stitchery, it is necessary to have the person learn by using the non-dominant hand. That is, I teach them to use the hand they do not normally use for embroidery. This helps the embroiderer to learn, as the beginner sewer might, with no preconceived notions. Once the technique is understood, in a matter of fifteen minutes or so, it is a very simple matter to transfer the needle to the dominant hand, because there is now also a visual reinforcement of how the needle is held and manipulated.

Remember: The needle is held sideways and the action is a scooping motion from the wrist. The thumb and index finger hold the needle, the middle finger functioning as a guide. (People with hand problems very successfully make their own adjustments.) It makes good sense when we are dealing with a taut fabric working surface and a half-circle needle, that what goes in must come out by itself—a stitch is completed in one motion. It is not necessary for the embroiderer to push the top of the needle up from the underside of the work as the needle will simply come out by itself. The idea is that once the needle is held between the thumb and forefinger with the middle finger as a pushing guide, the needle goes into the fabric, gets pushed through from the threaded end, and the hand then moves over and grasps at the middle of the needle to remove it from the fabric. In that same instant the needle is manipulated in the fingers by the middle finger in order to turn the needle to the right position for the next stitch. We are, in effect, making a full-circle motion of the needle. (See chronological illustrations.)

For the beginner there are many ways of handling the curved needle, but the primary idea is for the embroiderer to be comfortable. Some people prefer to have the hoop or frame lie flat on a hard surface in front of them for practicing. Others prefer to hold it perpendicularly with the opposite hand. Still others prefer to lean the frame up against the edge of the table where they are working. There are no hard-and-fast rules of thumb. For the embroiderer to be perfectly comfortable, it is necessary to find one's own way. If you prefer, however, to work on your lap, that is perfectly acceptable—although sooner or later you will certainly stitch your work to yourself! But it is then a simple matter to remove the stitches and start again.

When embroidering, since the work is done only from the surface with this needle, and since we never use knots, I suggest that a little x be made in order to anchor the beginning of a thread. Then the x can be covered with the embroidery. This method is ideal when working satin stitch, as the stitches cover over the little x very well. For long and short stitches, running stitches, back stitches, chain stitches, and split stitches take tiny running stitches in the opposite direction from which your work is progressing and then cover these tiny running stitches with stitchery. This is a method of concealing the tail of the thread as it is anchored in the fabric. Working over the anchored thread makes the back of the work come out as neat as the front of the work, and if there is a small amount of shrinkage in washing, the thread eases out and there are no dimples in the cloth. The only time you might take the needle to the back of the work is for catching the beginning of the thread in canvaswork embroidery; that is, if you do not wish to use a waste-knot technique. Unlike regular embroidery needles, stainless-steel surgical needles are carefully honed, and prepared of solid steel, and, in the process of being used, get sharper and better. One of the side benefits I found was that the work went much more quickly with this needle, that the stitches were much more even, and that people with deformities could adapt this needle to their own comforts and needs and find themselves embroidering if they have given up this fine art form years ago or have been afraid even to attempt it.

As far as I know, the only time that a surgical needle needs to be replaced is when it has been badly abused or lost. By badly abused I mean using a needle that is too thin for the work being done, as in the stitching of leather or heavy felt. For heavy materials a surgical clamp is used to push the needle in and to pull it out. The clamp can also pull a needle out of shape.

What is lovely about the curved needle is that one can acquire facility with both hands, since the needleworker who has learned with the non-dominant hand now acquires the ability to use two hands. This is very beneficial for the work and gives the needleworker a whole new way of executing stitchery.

To begin practicing the use of this needle, it is recommended that you use a piece of muslin as a doodle cloth, or a piece of waste canvas—or both. The idea is to practice with a sharp needle by starting first with running stitches. I suggest that you do several rows with the non-dominant hand. Next, try back stitches and then split stitches. It generally takes between five and twenty-five minutes to learn how to use the needle and it requires a bit of patience. Once some facility is acquired with the non-dominant hand, it is suggested that you switch to the dominant hand and try diagonal stitches on your doodle cloth. Then proceed to work on a piece of canvas, applying the same concept, using the blunt needle for canvaswork.

Other uses for the curved surgical needle are: filling in missing stitches, repairing a mounted embroidery, and as a finishing tool for many varieties of needlework.

The embroiderer should be aware that in the medical profession these needles are never used by hand. They are always used with a clamp so that medical friends and relations cannot necessarily show you how to use the curved needle. Sometimes they even resist the idea of using one of their tools in another area of expertise or for another profession. Generally the use of a clamp for this needle in embroidery is necessary when working with leather and with heavy, thick fabrics such as felt, or for layers of material that require some extra strength to pull the needle through.

Many surgical supply houses resent and are suspicious of embroiderers coming in and asking for needles. I suggest that you make inquiries through your local embroidery guild. Sooner or later you will come upon someone or some shop who either has them for sale or knows where you can get them. Generally, for embroidery, it is recommended that a $2\frac{1}{4}$-inch half-circle to a $2\frac{1}{2}$-inch half-circle sharp intestinal needle be used. The sharp embroidery needle also seems to be excellent for appliqué, patchwork, and quilting. For canvaswork it is generally recommended that a $2\frac{1}{4}$-inch half-circle to a $2\frac{1}{2}$-inch half-circle dull-tipped kidney needle be used.

15.
FINISHING TECHNIQUES

✳ ─────────────────────────── ✳

BEFORE AN EMBROIDERY is prepared for mounting or hanging, many decisions have to be made. The first thing we do is examine the embroidery. Next, we consider what kind of object we are going to mount and what kind of mount we need. What purpose will it serve? Does the embroidery need to appear larger than it actually is, or should it be finished in its actual size? Does it need matting? Will it require a frame, plain shadowbox, or what? Does it need protective glass in front of it against airborne pollutants and dust? Will glare pose a problem? What other choices are available? Is this object too large to be treated as a framed picture? Is it too small to mount as is, or must it have a mat to enlarge it? What material, colored matting board, or fabric should be used for this mat? Should the matting be complementary or contrasting? In making these decisions, always consider the use—*only*—of acid-free, inert materials so that you do not bring any acidic or deleterious materials in contact with the embroidery itself.

If the object only needs freshening, then it should be washed and blocked. The washing should be done in a mild soap solution. First, take the object and sandwich it between two pieces of nylon tulle or mesh and gently sponge through the embroidery with mild soap suds. Sponging through a mesh will prevent the fibers from napping by preventing any of them from being moved about while the gentle sponging action is taking place. The object should then be rinsed thoroughly under fresh cool water while it is still between the two pieces of mesh.

138.

Hopefully, the embroiderer has worked the embroidery on a hoop or on an artist's stretcher in order to keep it squared and straight. If the object is not worked on a frame or stretcher or hoop, it will be lopsided and uneven, and a lot of stress will have to be put on it to straighten it out. Because of the lopsidedness, in all likelihood it will then have to be affixed to a permanent stretcher and will not be able to be loose-hanging.

Ideally, every needleworker should have something on which to block the embroidery. In order to block a clean item that has been embroidered—whether worked on a canvas, a piece of linen, or a piece of cotton—the same procedure should be followed. Specifically, a piece of porous board material should be used, covered with contact paper. The board should be soft so that pins can go into it easily, while the contact paper makes it waterproof. Sometimes one is able to find contact paper in a checkerboard design; it is then easier for the embroiderer to line up the warps and wefts of the fabric against these checkered lines. Rustproof pins, generally available from your local notions store, should be used. Line up your warp and your weft very gently. Use the rustproof pins to hold the embroidery in place until the embroidery is dry. Definitely do *not* use an iron to make the object smooth, and do not machine dry. Ideally, the object should be straightened with the fingers while wet. Heat can not only damage the fibers but can also shrink the materials.

Once the object is dry, you have many different ways to do the mounting and framing. If you are concerned with the longevity of a piece of work that is being made, as with either a family heirloom or a commissioned project, you certainly should consider the kinds of materials to be used for the mounting and the hanging. Specifically, all your procedures should be reversible procedures. By reversible, I mean: no glue or adhesive tapes of any variety, no staples, and no materials that will bore holes or mutilate the embroidery in any way. In museology techniques, a bristol-board mount is used for items that will be framed. It is highly recommended that this acid-free pH-neutral board be covered with washed unbleached muslin and closely stitched to fit. New, fresh muslin should be washed with soap to remove the sizing and then washed with hot water and dried in a dryer, so that if there is any percentage of shrinkage, it should take place at this point. The board is covered with the muslin and stitched carefully with concealed stitches. In preparing the bristol board with the washed unbleached-muslin covering, be sure that the board is very tightly covered and that the ends are tucked in on the side of the closing in order that the surface on the reverse side will be

149. Following are mounting and hanging procedures:

A. The embroidery is ready for mounting on bristol board that has been covered with washed, unbleached muslin.

B. Bristol board covered tautly with washed, unbleached muslin and held closed with rustproof pins. Concealed stitches are used to keep the work neat.

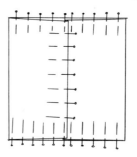

C. The edges of the muslin are tucked in very firmly to make straight and even corners. Less fabric works best for this.

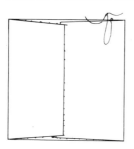

D. Matting techniques vary, depending on whether the embroidery is up to the edge of the covered backing board or whether there is space between the object and the edge of the frame.

E. Embroidery that has been laid on muslin-covered bristol board may be mounted on a larger surface of decorator fabric for matting.

EMBROIDERY ON MUSLIN COVERED BOARD

DECORATIVE MAT

F. A method for mounting a wall hanging is to stitch washed unbleached muslin to the top back of the hanging and let the muslin hang loose.

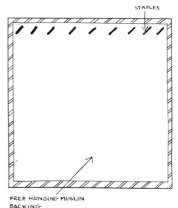

STAPLES

FREE HANGING MUSLIN BACKING

G. Stitch the soft side of the Velcro to the backing so that if the Velcro touches the surface of the needlework there is no danger of damage. The negative part of the Velcro is staple-gunned to the wall or to a board affixed to the wall.

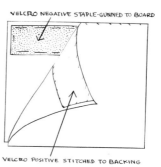

VELCRO NEGATIVE STAPLE-GUNNED TO BOARD

VELCRO POSITIVE STITCHED TO BACKING

perfectly smooth for mounting the embroidery. When mounting the new embroidery, the edges should be turned in and laid flat so that they are concealed between the mounting board and the embroidery itself. Using rustproof pins, make sure to get a perfect fit, and use concealed stitching.

Once this is done, the embroidery can be affixed to the covered muslin board, also with concealed stitching all around. Despite the color of the embroidery, the stitching should be done in white mercerized cotton thread only. That done, the object can then be treated in many different ways for mounting, by adding matting and the framing of your choice. If a colored matting is desired, then the object can be mounted in many different ways. An artist's stretcher—on which mounting board is stapled or on which fabric is stretched and stapled to the reverse side with a staple gun—can be used. The embroidery can then be stitched to that ground fabric with a concealed stitch; or, if it is necessary to use glue, the back of the muslin can be glued to the mount. I would like to discourage the use of glue in order to reduce as far as possible the risk of getting glue on the embroidery.

You may prefer to have the fabric stretched over a piece of three-ply newsboard instead of wood or a mounting. The decision is always up to the embroiderer who is doing the work. With this final mounting, we are not concerned with reversible procedures because at any time you are tired of the mount or it is worn and you desire to replace it, then it is a simple matter of merely carefully removing the stitches that hold the embroidery to its mounting board. Everything else can then be disposed of. Hopefully, the embroidery will still be in perfect condition.

To fit a frame to the outside of the mat is a simple procedure. Using a protective glass is not as simple a matter, since it is necessary to keep the embroidery breathing and to see that the glass does not touch the surface of the object. It is recommended that, in order to keep the glass away from the embroidery, a wedge of matting board or wood filler be inserted between the glass and the mat. Once the object is laid into its frame with the filler keeping the glass off the surface, the back of the frame should

H. and I. A wood dowel covered in muslin may also be used for a hanging when a muslin sleeve is prepared on the backing material.

DOWEL COVERED IN MUSLIN

DOWEL WITH MUSLIN SLEEVE

then be kept open and not covered with paper. Preferably, a piece of muslin should be staple-gunned to the top of the back of the frame. This serves as a dust cover and it also allows the embroidery to breathe. When this dust cover gets dirty, it can easily be removed and thrown away or it can be washed and replaced. Variations on this kind of framing can be done at the discretion of the embroiderer, always remembering to protect the embroidery from harm and remembering that the embroidery itself should not be involved in any procedure that is not reversible.

As for wall hangings, it is advisable that they be kept away from radiators because of the heat and because they attract dust. It is not advisable to hang unprotected textiles and embroideries in the kitchen, or even in the bathroom, where there may be too much moisture and/or too much heat. Framed embroideries are protected from the front with a glass and at the back with a piece of muslin as well. For a wall hanging we can only protect the back. Interestingly enough, for whatever scientific reasons may be involved, any object that hangs on the wall seems to attract dust. The wall itself may remain clean, but the area around or behind the object seems to accumulate dust. It is for this reason that we use a protective lining. The backing fabric for a wall hanging should be a simple piece of muslin, twill, or duck made of cotton. Careful measurements should be taken of the hanging so that the backing material can be cut generously, with allowances for a sleeve at the top—through which a covered wood dowel will go—as well as allowances for generous seams on the sides and bottom. This backing fabric should be washed with soap to remove the sizing, and then washed in plain water to remove soap residue. The seam and sleeve can be sewn by machine.

The backing should then be affixed, by hand, to the embroidery hanging by stitching the top and a few inches down on either side. White mercerized cotton should be used, with concealed stitching. If it is desired that the wall hanging not be hung with a wooden dowel in a prepared sleeve, then a Velcro fastening may be used. In all cases, the lining for a wall hanging is affixed to the top of the wall hanging. The rest is left to hang loose. Once the lining is affixed to the top, the soft side of the Velcro is sewn to the backing by using a method of stitching that goes right through the front of the embroidery. If this is done properly, over the warps and between the wefts, the affixing stitchery will not be visible from the front. (See Illustration 149.) It is recommended that the negative part of the Velcro be staple-gunned to a piece of wood for the wall mount.

Depending on the size of the wall hanging, a piece of lumber can be used for a lightweight hanging. If the object is heavier, you can go on to use a piece of lumber $1'' \times 2''$ ($2\frac{1}{2}$ cm. $\times$ 5 cm.) for a medium-weight hanging, and you may even use a piece of lumber $2'' \times 4''$ (5 cm. $\times$ 10 cm.) for a very heavy wall hanging. The piece of wood should be drilled with three or four holes through it in order that construction nails can be used for mounting on the wall. The idea is that a piece of wood can be slipped onto these construction nails and be easily removed. The negative part of the Velcro is staple-gunned to the piece of wood.

For the physical act of hanging it is advisable to take the textile with the positive Velcro on it, fold it in half, and, beginning at the center of the wood with the negative, rub your fingers to the right and then to the left across the face of the textile to affix it to its wall mount. It should hang with ease and with an even distribution of weight. Minor adjustments can be made as well. The average object hangs very successfully with a Velcro of three-quarter to one-inch thickness. For larger and heavier textiles, a 2-inch (approximately 5 cm.) Velcro is recommended.

After it is hung, the sides and the bottom of the backing material need to be dealt with. Let the hanging find its own level for a few days before finishing the edges of the backing fabric. It is advisable that the hems for the sides and bottoms be turned facing the wall so that only flat fabric touches the back of the textile. The reasons for letting the fabric hang out are that loomed pieces and embroidered pieces very often are not squared (sometimes even canvas and linen are not squared either). If it is allowed to hang for a few days to find its own level, you will note that the seams may be different on each side of the piece. The practice of letting it hang for a few days prevents the job of seaming from needing to be done more than once.

A DEFINITION OF
NEEDLEWORKING TERMS

Needlework, or Embroidery, is a general term to describe a technique whereby a needle and a thread are passed through a woven fabric to create a surface stitch. It is, also, an art form sometimes referred to as needle painting and surface embellishment. "Found" objects and needle weaving may be added or applied to needlework to give dimension.

Appliqué is a method of applying small pieces of fabric to another fabric surface with stitches that hold the pieces in place.

Canvaswork (erroneously sometimes called "needlepoint," which is a lacemaking term) includes gros point and petit point. It may be worked in wool, silk, linen, or cotton on canvas as well as with synthetic fibers in a large variety of stitches.

Cotton embroidery is the working of floss or perle cotton to a cotton or linen ground fabric.

Crewel is the embroidery of wool on linen.

Quilting is a method of placing padding between two pieces of fabric and stitching the two together, usually in a pattern, to give a stuffed or quilted effect.

Silk and metal thread needlework is considered to be the crème de la crème of embroidery, in which silk threads are worked and metal threads of endless varieties are applied in a couching technique. It is traditional for ecclesiastical embroidery and is a very painstaking procedure.

Stumpwork is an early English method of applying small wood stumps to fabric and embroidering over them or painting them to give dimension to the work.

Three-dimensional needlework is raised appliqué objects or stuffed and raised motifs applied to a fabric surface to give it a three-dimensional element.

Tapestry is weaving on a loom, not needlework. The vertical thread is called the warp and the horizontal thread the weft. A shuttle is used to pass the wefts under and over the warps. Since no needle and thread are used to create a surface stitch, this is not a needlework/embroidery technique.

144.

A BIBLIOGRAPHY

Angel, Rabbi Marc D. *The Jews of Rhodes: The History of a Sephardic Community*. New York: Sepher-Hermon Press, Inc.; 1978.

"Armenian, Jewish or Arab Lace," *Embroidery* magazine. London: Embroiderer's Guild of London; date unknown.

Ashkenazi, Shmuel, and Dov Yarden. *Otzar Roshei Teivoth*. Jerusalem: Reuven Moss, Publisher; 1976.

Avi-Yonah, Michael, and Zvi Baras. *The World History of the Jewish People*, Vol. II: *The Herodian Period*. New Brunswick, N.J.: Rutgers University Press; 1975.

Barnett, R. D., editor. *Catalogue of the Jewish Museum, London*. London: New York Graphic Society, Ltd.; 1974.

Bialer, Yehudah L. *Jewish Life in Art and Tradition*. New York: G. P. Putnam's Sons; 1976.

Cohen, Rev. Dr. A., editor. *The Psalms*. London and Bournemouth: Soncino Press; 1950.

Davidowitz, David. *Ketuba: Jewish Marriage Contracts through the Ages*. Tel Aviv: E. Lewin-Epstein, Ltd., Publishers; 1968.

Deplanche, A., editor. *Dentelles et Broderies Tunisiennes*. Paris: 1931.

Encyclopaedia Judaica. Jerusalem: Keter Publishing House, Jerusalem, Ltd.; 1972.

"Fabric of Jewish Life." New York: Jewish Museum; 1977.

Finch, Karen, O.B.E., and Greta Putnam. *Caring for Textiles*. New York: Watson-Guptill Publications; 1977.

Goodenough, Erwin R. *Jewish Symbols of the Greco-Roman Period*, Vols. IX, X, and XI. New York: Bollingen Foundation, Pantheon Books; 1964.

Grossman, Grace Cohen. *The Jews of Yemen*. Chicago: Spertus College of Judaica Press; 1976.

Horowitz, Edward. *How the Hebrew Language Grew*. New York: Ktav Publishing House; 1967.

Journal of Jewish Art, The, Vols. I, II, III, and IV. Chicago, Ill.: Spertus College of Judaica Press; 1974, 1975, 1977.

Kampf, Avram. *Contemporary Synagogue Art*. New York: Union of American Hebrew Congregations; 1966.

Landay, Jerry M. *Silent Cities, Sacred Stones*. New York: McCall Publishing Company; 1971.

Landsberger, Franz. *A History of Jewish Art*. Cincinnati: Union of American Hebrew Congregations; 1946.

Leene, J. E. *Textile Conservation*. Washington, D.C.: Smithsonian Institution; 1972.

Mackie, Louise W. *Spain—Selections from the Textile Museum* (accompanied by 35 mm slides). Washington, D.C.: The Textile Museum; 1978.

May, Florence Lewis. *Hispanic Lace and Lace Making*. New York: Hispanic Society of America; 1939.

May, Florence Lewis. *Rugs of Spain and Morocco* (accompanied by microfiche). Hispanic Society of America. Chicago and London: University of Chicago Press; 1977.

Muller-Lancet, Aviva. *Elements in Costume and Jewellry Specific to the Jews of Morocco*. Jerusalem: The Israel Museum; 1976.

Muller-Lancet, Aviva. *On Judaic Embroidery of the City of San'a*. Jerusalem: The Israel Museum; 1964.

Narkiss, Bezalel, editor. *Hebrew Illuminated Manuscripts*. Jerusalem: Keter Publishing House Ltd.; 1969.

Roth, Cecil. *Jewish Art*. Greenwich, Conn.: New York Graphic Society, Ltd.; 1971.

Shahn, Ben. *The Alphabet of Creation: An Ancient Legend from the Zohar*. New York: Schocken Books; 1965.

Siegel, R., and M. and S. Strassfeld, editors. *The Jewish Catalog: A Do It Yourself Kit*. Philadelphia: The Jewish Publication Society of America; 1974.

Singer, Isadore, editor. *The Jewish Encyclopedia*. New York: Ktav Publishing House Inc.; 1904.

Spier, Arthur, editor. *The Comprehensive Hebrew Calendar*. New York: Behrman House, Inc., Publishers; 1952.

Stern, Dr. M., editor. *The Five Books of Moses*. New York: Star Hebrew Book Co.

Toby, L. F. *The Art of Hebrew Lettering*. Tel Aviv: Cosmopolite Ltd.; 1975.

Volavkova, Hana. *Synagogue Treasures of Bohemia and Moravia*. Prague: Sfinx; 1949.

Wischnitzer, Mark. *A History of Jewish Crafts and Guilds*. New York: Jonathan David, Publishers; 1965.

Yadin, Yigael. *Bar Kokhba*. New York: Random House; 1971.

Yadin, Yigael. *Masada: Herod's Fortress and the Zealot's Last Stand*. New York: Random House; 1966.

Index